Sensi

MW01488760

by
James G. Poitras

with Articles
by
Bruce A. Howell

Global Missions Edition

@2012 United Pentecostal Church International

Library of Congress Cataloging-in-Publication Data

Poitras, James.

Sensing God's direction / by James G. Poitras with articles by Bruce A. Howell. -- Global missions ed.

p. cm.

ISBN 978-0-7577-4397-9

1. Christian life. 2. God (Christianity)--Will. 3. Discernment (Christian theology) I. Howell, Bruce A. II. Title.

BV4509.5.P64 2012

248.4--dc23

2012031368

Sensing God's Direction

by

James G. Poitras

with Articles

by

Bruce A. Howell

Sensing God's direction: Why does it cause such brain pain and so much worthless worry? Too often we see it as an ultimate destination, not realizing it is a continuous journey. We erroneously envision ourselves being led through a huge maze or plopped down and told, "The puzzle of your life is in one thousand pieces. Put it together!"

God is not messing with our minds. He is not playing hide-and-seek. We are not pawns or players in His mystery thriller. He longs to provide us the direction we need. He orders our footsteps. And He reveals His will in the increments best suited for us. The process unfolds according to the Master's master plan. The will of God does not have to be a mystery. It is like a winding road depicted as an "S." As you start out on the trip, you can only see as far as the headlights shine—to the bend in the road. Once you travel around the curve, you can see further.

Since we are taking a trip together you may want to know a little about the journey, stopping off places, direction markers and so forth. Throughout this book these will be indicated by various "S" words including:

- ▲ Souls
- ▲ Solitude
- ▲ Sensitivity
- ▲ Surrender
- ▲ Sacrifice
- ▲ Submission
- ▲ Spiritual Transformation
- ▲ Scars
- ▲ Stains
- ▲ Sanctification
- ▲ Seek and Search
- ▲ Spotlight
- ▲ Story
- ▲ Seasons
- ▲ Situations
- ▲ Seer
- ▲ Sensibility
- ▲ Satisfaction
- ▲ Study
- ▲ Stewardship
- ▲ Service/Servanthood
- ▲ Strengths
- ▲ Suffering
- ▲ Specific
- ▲ Selected
- ▲ Steadfast
- ▲ Stickability
- ▲ Step
- ▲ Strategy
- ▲ Seasoned Supervision
- ▲ Stand Still

"God has made everything beautiful for its own time. He has planted eternity in the human heart, but even so, people cannot see the whole scope of God's work from beginning to end" (Ecclesiastes 3:11, *New Living Translation*).

Knowing the will of God is one thing. Doing it is entirely different. George Truett said, "To know the will of God is our greatest knowledge. To do the will of God is our greatest achievement." A good place for us to begin is with a commitment not only to sense God's will, but to satisfy God's will. Not just to know it, but to do it.

A young missionary said it was much easier dreaming about being a missionary than it was actually being one. Likely those called in any area of God's kingdom would readily testify, "Doing God's will is lots of plain old work!"

Leon Chambers concluded that the will of God is a term "most often used to refer to God's guidance." It is not a matter of finding God's will. His will is never lost. It is revealed.

God reveals the will of God.
We discover the will of God.
We prove the will of God (Romans 12:2).
Others confirm the will of God.
We obey the will of God.
An Italian proverb states, "What God wills, I will."

God says, "I have a plan for your life" (Jeremiah 29:11). You respond, "Great, Lord. What is it?"

A Personal Note from the Author

Hold on! We're moving fast. I better tell you a little about the author. That's me, Jim Poitras. I was converted in 1979, while in university, when Lynne, a high school girl, witnessed to me. She is now a missionary in Guatemala. I was nurtured and cared for by the Fred Thompson family. Their son, Brad, is not only a close friend but also a missionary to Guatemala. My pastor was a mission's lover. So I didn't have a chance. In 1983, after three years in the church, and at the ripe old age of twenty-two (well, one week before I turned twenty-three), I went on the AIM program to Nigeria, West Africa.

This booklet contains some of the things I have learned about sensing God's will over the past quarter of a century. It is hard to believe I have been doing the missions thing for over twenty-eight years. My wife, Linda, (before she became my wife) was one of the first Associates in Missions (AIMers) endorsed in 1981 as part of the newly established AIM program from Global Missions.

"Why is he telling us this? I thought this was a lesson booklet." The answer is simple. I wanted you to know the reason for this epistle. I give glory to God for selecting me to be part of His huge end-time harvest. I am glad I sensed His direction—and obeyed it. I dedicate this writing to all Associates in Missions and young people embarking on the Next Step program. You are my heroes. I hope something written in the following pages will help as you not only sense God's direction but also step out into it.

I admit it. I am soft on missions! After so many years of missionary service in Africa, and now as the director of Education/AIM for

Global Missions, tears still flow when I hear songs like "People Need the Lord" (by Greg Nelson and Phil McHugh). A sense of mission still wells up when I see the parade of missionary flag-bearers march in during our general conference missions service. Globes and maps of the world decorate my office, signifying the interior décor of my heart as well. They constantly remind me of my destiny in life.

One or two disclaimers: It may seem like there is a lot of emphasis on missions. That is intentional. For this I offer no apology. God can place you anywhere in His kingdom. If He is not directing you toward world missions, use the principles given in this booklet anyway. They work. No matter which way you're heading, I am persuaded the Lord of the harvest is always directing His children toward winning the lost world! With that, ends most of my first person references. I will be switching to the third person mode to make it easy for others to teach this resource. Additionally, the articles written by Bruce A. Howell, for the most part, were written to missionaries. The scope of this book surpasses that since every effort is made to provide helpful guidance to anyone seeking God's will.

Back to *Sensing God's Direction*. Enjoy the journey!

Souls

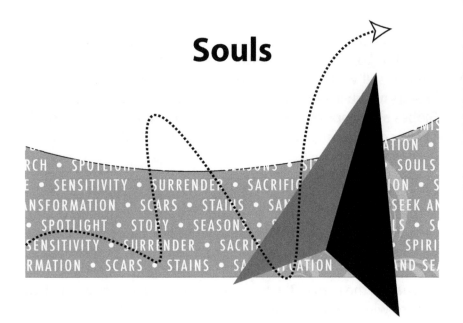

Some may speculate that souls are a strange place to start a discourse about sensing God's direction. Not really. It makes God-sense. In fact, it was the basis of Jesus' final directions. Global Missions Director Bruce Howell said, "It's all about souls! Souls rescued. Souls readied."

People speak of the "fair market value" of a manufactured product or its "retail value." They talk of "wholesale value" or "trade-in value." Have you ever heard of "soul value"? Nothing is more valuable than a person's soul.

Studies have determined that the monetary value of mineral and chemical elements found in the human body is less than one dollar. Our most valuable asset is our skin. Based on the selling price of cowhide, the value of an average person's skin is about $3.50. Total monetary value per person equals $4.50. But we are made up of more than oxygen, calcium, sodium, iron, zinc, copper, and about fourteen other minerals and chemicals. We are body, soul, and spirit. We have eternal value. We are priceless. We are not for sale. We have already been bought by the precious blood of the crucified Lamb. Souls last for eternity!

We need to invest our lives with eternity in view. God places great value on a lost soul (John 3:16). It was for this reason Jesus came into the world. "For the Son of man is come to seek and to save that which was lost" (Luke 19:10). In one short sentence Jesus described His purpose—to seek and to save. He also explained His target group—the lost. We remain on the earth to finish the task. Before He left, He said, "As my Father hath sent me, even so send I you" (John 20:21). There are two things you can do on earth that cannot be done in heaven: sin and win the lost. I think we both know which we are supposed to be doing. Right?

"Today . . . people will go to heaven, and people will go to hell. The percentage of people going to heaven and the percentage of people going to hell today is determined by how well you did your job yesterday. If you remember heaven today, it will help someone avoid hell tomorrow." *(Primary Purpose)*

"What are You Going to Do?"
by
Bruce A. Howell

Night after night, our missionaries stand in pulpits wrestling to find the words to communicate their burden for over seven billion people in our lost world. Every 4.1 seconds another soul is born on this planet. There are over 100,000 more lost people in the world today than yesterday. Statistics have a way of falling short of imparting vision and impacting precious saints on comfortable pews.

Facing a sleepless night? Instead of counting sheep, count souls. One lost soul. Two lost souls. Three lost souls. Four lost souls. Five lost souls. Six lost souls. Seven lost souls. Eventually you will fall asleep or spend months counting lost souls. But that illustration falls short of reality.

William Booth, founder of Salvation Army, once remarked, "Most Christian ministries would like to send their recruits to Bible college for four or five years. I would like to send our recruits to hell for five minutes. That would do more than anything else to prepare them for a lifetime of compassionate ministry."

It is not possible to take a five-minute excursion to Hell, but it is possible to visit the local mortuary and/or cemetery. Give me a choice between a visit to a cemetery, mortuary, or a restaurant, the food place wins hands down.

So let's go with a trip to the restaurant—an after-church favorite event. One of our UPCI missionary families, traveling on deputation, accompanied a pastor and his wife to a local restaurant. On the way to their table, they passed a man who called out, "Are you Christians?" The missionary quickly confirmed that he was indeed a Christian. The man responded, "I am a sinner. What are you going to do about it?" He reemphasized his point, "I see you are here with friends and probably have come for a good time. Just remember. I am a sinner. What are you going to do about it?" The missionary put hunger on hold, sat down with the man, listened intently as he rehearsed his life, and then unfolded the gospel to him.

Stop! That brings things to reality. Statistics bore us. Counting souls puts us to sleep. Quotations or a trip to the cemetery fall short of imparting vision. The restaurant rendezvous articulates it best. "I am lost. I am a sinner. What are you going do about it?" That testimony is shared throughout our world—across the street at a local restaurant or across the seas in our developing world. The helpless beggar on the streets of Calcutta, India, or the entrepreneur in Los Angeles, California, share the same testimony, "I am lost. I am a sinner. What are you going to do about it?" They also share the same fate, unless we are willing to do something about it.

I will strive to reach them with our life-changing message of hope and salvation. I will pray that the Lord of the harvest will send forth workers to evangelize our world (and do my part to see it happen). I will faithfully give to world missions. I will go and do as the Lord leads. I've answered the question. Now it's your turn.

Outside the doors of your church and home is a world filled with people. They are lost. They are sinners. "What are you going to do about it?"

Only for souls my life's work shall be,
Only for souls till death shall set us free,
I'll strive as those striving after earth's goals,
Only for souls, only for souls.
(Author Unknown)

Solitude

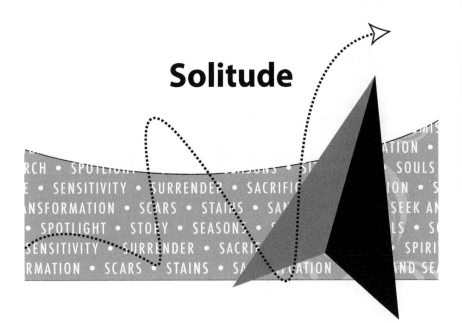

It is easier to hear the voice of God in solitude. Here we can give our undivided, undistracted, full attention. Some hear God best in their prayer closet. Others at the church altar. Others hear His voice loudest with the backdrop of crashing waves or in the silence beside a still lake. Others hear best observing from the pinnacle of a mountain.

"For this reason we also, from the day we heard of it, have not ceased to pray and make [special] request for you, [asking] that you may be filled with the full (deep and clear) knowledge of His will in all spiritual wisdom [in comprehensive insight into the ways and purposes of God] and in understanding and discernment of spiritual things (Colossians 1:9, Amplified Bible).

How do we find out what God wants? Simple! Talk to Him. Ask for the mind of Christ. "For who hath known the mind of the Lord, that he may instruct him? But we have the mind of Christ" (I Corinthians 2:16). "For my thoughts are not your thoughts, neither are your ways my ways, saith the LORD. For as the heavens are higher than your ways, and my thoughts than your thoughts" (Isaiah 55:8-9).

Jesus set the example for us. "And in the morning, rising up a great while before day, he went out, and departed into a solitary place, and there prayed" (Mark 1:35). He also taught us the way. "But when you pray, go away by yourself, shut the door behind you, and pray to your Father secretly" (Matthew 6:6, NLT).

There is an old song that says, "Shut in with God in a secret place." When Jesus approached important decisions, He prayed. When tempted, He prayed (Matthew 4). Before selecting His twelve disciples, He prayed all night. "He went out into a mountain to pray, and continued all night in prayer to God" (Luke 6:12). When He was about to be betrayed, He prayed; "And he went a little farther, and fell on his face and prayed, O my Father, if it be possible, let this cup pass from me: nevertheless not as I will, but as thou wilt" (Matthew 26:39).

William Carey is considered the father of modern missions. He had an immense burden for the lost. As a young man, he worked in a shoe cobbler's shop. He saved discarded bits and pieces of shoe leather and made a makeshift globe. He sketched in ink the outlines of the continents and various countries on his crude leather globe. It is said that Carey's tears of intercession for the world literally blurred the outlines of the nations on his handmade globe. He became a missionary to India and changed the course of mission's history throughout the world.

Are You Connected?
by
Laurissa Wolfram

I work at a computer help desk; and over the past few years, I have heard some pretty crazy things. A friend of mine told me about a time when he suggested that a client "warm-boot" her computer, which basically means forcing the computer to restart without actually turning it off. Well, the lady took him literally and put her computer in the oven. Then there was the person who came in wondering why his computer wasn't working. When we took it apart, we were surprised to see it was inhabited by a nice little colony of ants, who had set up camp beneath his keyboard. Brings a whole new meaning to "my computer has a bug," doesn't it?

But my favorite (and one of the most frequent) is when someone calls in a panic, requesting someone to come to their office immediately because their computer won't turn on. Of course, when the analyst we send out comes back smiling and shaking his head we always know: they didn't have the machine plugged in.

Sometimes our lives are like that. We try and we try, but we become frustrated when things don't work out. We think we're doing all the right things and can't understand why all our efforts seem to be in vain. But after sitting there, dejected and discouraged, we realize we're not plugged into the power source. We can push all the right buttons and flip all the switches, but none of that will matter unless the power is flowing!

God is like our power source. His strength and life gives us what we need to function and survive. Without Him, we're just going through the motions. So the next time you feel like things just aren't working out the way they should, step back and think. Are you connected to the source?

There is something else we should do in secret. Fasting gets us out of the way so we can clearly hear God.

"For thus saith the Lord GOD, the Holy One of Israel; In returning and rest shall ye be saved; in quietness and in confidence shall be your strength" (Isaiah 30:15).

"Moreover when ye fast, be not, as the hypocrites, of a sad countenance: for they disfigure their faces, that they may appear unto men to fast. Verily I say unto you, They have their reward" (Matthew 6:16).

Fasting expresses our seriousness about knowing God's will. It is advisable to fast before any major change in your life or ministry. The early church did. "As they ministered to the Lord, and fasted, the Holy Ghost said, Separate me Barnabas and Saul whereunto I have called them" (Acts 13:2).

Fasting strengthens prayers. "And Cornelius said, Four days ago I was fasting until this hour, and at the ninth hour I prayed in my house, and behold, a man stood before me in bright clothing, and said, Cornelius, thy prayer is heard, and thine alms are had in remembrance in the sight of God" (Acts 10:30-31).

Fasting is important when one needs to seek the Lord. "And I set my face unto the Lord God, to seek by prayer and supplications, with fasting, and sackcloth, and ashes" (Daniel 9:3).

"And Jehoshaphat feared, and set himself to seek the Lord, and proclaimed a fast throughout all Judah. And Judah gathered themselves together, to ask help of the Lord; even out of all the cities of Judah they came to seek the Lord" (II Chronicles 20:3-4).

Elmer Towns suggested that if there is a place where God has met with you in the past, then that is a good place for you to go to pray and fast.

There are three measured steps to fasting:

- ▲ Vow to God that you will fast.
- ▲ Prepare for the fast.
- ▲ Fulfill your resolution.

You might have missed the implication here. Sensing God's direction? Seeking His will? What next? Perhaps a short fast is in order.

Sensitivity

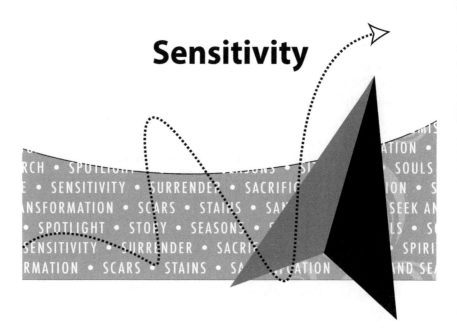

"As they ministered to the Lord, and fasted, the Holy Ghost said..." (Acts 13:2).

How do you know when God is speaking to you? Roger Barrier in *Listening to the Voice of God* explains, "Ever had an experience where deep down inside you just knew what to do; where God gave you impressions, encouragement, and advice?" He calls that place his "knower." "Deep down in my knower, I knew what God wanted." Barrier defines his "knower" as "this place deep inside where I know God speaks . . . it is there that I have heard the voice of God."

D. Martin Lloyd-Jones said, "... God sometimes answers directly in our spirit. The prophet said, 'I will wait and see what he will say in me.' God speaks to me by speaking in me... He can impress something upon our spirits in an unmistakable manner. We find ourselves unable to get away from an impression that is on our mind and heart." Perhaps this is what Elijah experienced when God spoke in a "still small voice" (I Kings 19:12). Some call it an inner compulsion (I Corinthians 9:16), inner peace (Isaiah 26:3), inner voice, inner feeling, inner impression, inner aspiration (I Timothy 3:1), and/or inner desire (Psalms 37:4).

The early preachers cultivated sensitivity to the Spirit. The Spirit spoke to them and through them many times. "Then the Spirit said unto Philip, Go near, and join thyself to this chariot" (Acts 8:29). "And the spirit bade me go with them, nothing doubting. Moreover these six brethren accompanied me, and we entered into the man's house" (Acts 11:12).

Who is leading you? It is important to be led by the Spirit. "For as many as are led by the Spirit of God, they are the sons of God" (Romans 8:14).

The Bible is the authority. What we sense from the Spirit should be in conformity with the Word of God. "Thy word is a lamp unto my feet, and a light unto my path" (Psalms 119:105).

We hear from the Spirit when we concentrate on the things of the Spirit, when we bring our thoughts into captivity (II Corinthians 10:5). Did you hear from God? How can you tell? Four things usually speak to our minds:

- ▲ Spirit
- ▲ Self
- ▲ Satan
- ▲ World

Which one are you listening to? God's voice is not the only voice that speaks to us. How can we distinguish between His voice and Satan's? Again Roger Barrier comes to the rescue. He suggests that God speaks to our innermost spirit. Satan and the flesh speak to the mind.

God speaks with a gentle leading. He does not push, drive, or dominate. Satan places people in bondage. God's voice provides freedom. God tends to speak when you are seeking Him (Jeremiah 29:12-13). He gives specific directions.

When the flesh and Satan speak, it feels as if things are out of control. When God speaks, you feel everything is under control. God speaks with 100 percent truth that can be tested by the Word of God. Satan brings confusion. God's voice leads to deep peace (Philippians 4:7).

We need to be sensitive to the voice of the Spirit. "My sheep hear my voice, and I know them, and they follow me" (John 10:27). Paul testified, "For I determined not to know anything among you, save Jesus Christ, and him crucified" (I Corinthians 2:2).

The key to knowing God's will is knowing God and His voice. "And the sheep hear his voice: and he calleth his own sheep by name, and leadeth them out. And when he putteth forth his own sheep, he goeth before them, and the sheep follow him: for they know his voice. And a stranger will they not follow, but will flee from him: for they know not the voice of strangers" (John 10:3-5).

The Baby!
by
Linda Revell Poitras

I was the baby . . . and they treated me that way. With a sister thirteen years older and a brother seven years my senior, I was their live baby doll. My sister took me into her room to take care of me in the night. (She was getting ready for motherhood a few short years ahead of time. Her first baby came when I was nine years old.)

My brother came home from school and taught his two-year-old sister what he had already mastered at school. Before my second birthday, he had taught me to spell and write my name, write my ABCs, count and write to ten. (He was practicing early for his lifelong teaching career.) After all, I was the baby. . . .

Any and everything I needed was mine. Daddy (my pastor) and Mama (my best friend, confidant, Sunday school teacher, and dress designer) were quick to see to that. I loved them both so much.

They taught me to love God's Word and that His will was the most important thing I could seek for my life. But I was still the baby. . . .

Growing up in a small town and attending the local schools, I never traveled further than from Alabama to Florida for vacations and family outings. I was not very adventurous. Graduating from university with a bachelor's degree in music education, I worked in schools near my home giving private voice and piano lessons . . . being the baby was still me.

Church was a major part of my life . . . and finding God's will for me *was paramount. The summer after college graduation, I attended senior youth camp where God began dealing with me about going . . . somewhere.*

After a miraculous provision of needed funds, I flew . . . for the very first time. That trip in 1978 with the International Youth Corps (currently called Apostolic Youth Corps) to Alaska changed my life. It taught me God does have a plan for each of us; and when He speaks, He always provides . . . especially for His babies.

That was the start of a four-year struggle. Change . . . and giving up my pampered life . . . was something I dreaded. Stop being the baby . . . do I want to? Where was God leading me? When God calls He not only provides, He gives clear direction.

When direction came, God confirmed His will with my parents, family, church leaders, and just about everyone I knew. He spoke loud and clear . . . no mistaking that voice. "You are going to Nigeria." Where? I knew it was in Africa, but that was about all I understood when I boarded that plane in July 1981. Still the baby, but a chosen one for a specific purpose. God was leading, and I had made up my mind to listen and follow. The baby was growing up . . . finally.

When I left Nigeria after three months in the bush (literally), it wasn't the pretty scenery or beautiful beaches that pulled on my heartstrings. . . because there weren't any. It wasn't the pleasant climate or comfortable living conditions that brought the throat-strangling tears. Nigeria was hot, humid, and dusty. But God's love reaching out through my hands and heart to souls who had never heard His name . . . they had a stranglehold on my life, and they still do. So I returned again and again. That same desire and purpose led our family from Nigeria to Ghana.

What did I find by following God's call? A whole new way of living, a different view of life with new priorities, thinner blood (living in this tropical heat for so long), and a husband! Yep, God sent a young man to Nigeria all the way from Canada. It was time for this baby to really grow up . . . so I did.

More than thirty years after following that first leading away from all that security (remember I was the baby?), I am still listening for His call. During the time while I waited for approval and all the red tape of my AIM application, God gave me a song. It still means a lot to me (baby or not) because "My Soul Heard God's Call!"

For my soul heard God's call, and I remembered His voice;
It was a call for my heart and my life and my time,
and it gave me a choice.
I could listen and heed, or merrily go my own way;
I'm so glad I did choose, my life for Jesus to use, each and every day!

Surrender

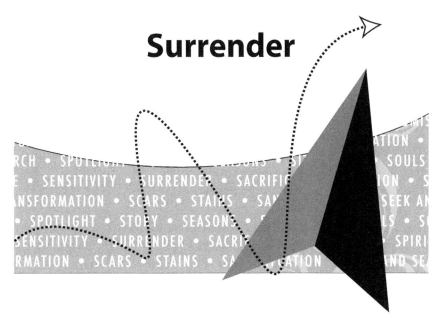

An old Nigerian chorus goes like this: "Jesus surrendered His life for me. What have I done for Him?" You must first make yourself available. Be open for God to reveal His will.

What Can I Give Him?
by
Bruce A. Howell

"And she brought forth her firstborn son, and wrapped him in swaddling clothes, and laid him in a manger; because there was no room for them in the inn" (Luke 2:7).

There is a villain in almost every good story. In the Christmas narrative the scoundrel is the calloused, cruel innkeeper. He turns the needy couple away. Hello! She is about to have a baby. How could he be so heartless? He deserves the rap for his nonchalant attitude. He is inconsiderate, insensible, and insensitive. He is responsible for the King of kings being born in a stable (or so the traditional story goes).

Wait a minute. First of all, let us not forget God's plan. He was in control (then and now) of every circumstance. Perhaps the innkeeper wasn't so thoughtless after all. He never was the rascal. Instead of sending the young couple away, he offered the only available space in his inn—the stable. He gave the best he had to offer.

> *What can I give Him, poor as I am?*
> *If I were a shepherd, I would bring a lamb;*
> *If I were a wise man, I would do my part;*
> *Yet what can I give Him?*
> *Give Him my heart!*
> *(C. Rossetti)*

God never requires anything more from us than we are able to give. You may sometimes feel you have little to offer. In the face of huge financial needs, you may lament your meager means. You may struggle with the language or stumble through cultural expectations. Gripped with feelings of being ill-equipped and inadequate, you may wonder, "Why am I here?" Occasionally you may even sigh, "What can I give Him?"

God has placed you in His vineyard. He has a master plan for your life. You are right where He wants you. His strength is made perfect in your weakness. He is making you into the Christian you need to be. Give Him the best gift of all—yourself.

Your heart must be right before Him.

- ▲ "And ye shall seek me, and find me, when you search for me with all your heart" (Jeremiah 29:13).
- ▲ "Search me, O God, know my heart: try me, and know my thoughts" (Psalm 139:23).
- ▲ "Not with eye service, as men pleasers: but as the servants of Christ, doing the will of God from the heart; with good will doing service, as to the Lord, and not to men" (Ephesians 6:6-7).
- ▲ "And let us run with endurance the race that God has set before us" (Hebrews 12:1, NLT).

The race is "set before us." It has already been decided. Stay in your lane!

Charles Swindoll said, "Prayer is connecting with God in order to transfer His will into your life. It is collaborating with God to accomplish His goals." He also added, "God never hides His will. If we seek direction, He delights in providing it." It is time to surrender by pulling yourself onto the altar. Once in a while you will slide off. Drag yourself back on.

Sacrifice

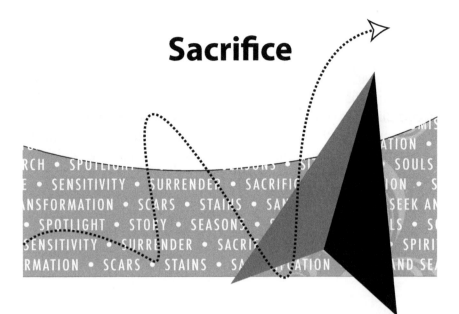

We are called upon to present ourselves as living sacrifices, to give up our lives as we continue living them. "I beseech you therefore, brethren, by the mercies of God, that ye present your bodies a living sacrifice, holy, acceptable unto God, which is your reasonable service. And be not conformed to this world: but be ye transformed by the renewing of your mind, that ye may prove what is that good, and acceptable, and perfect, will of God" (Romans 12:1-2).

Death Just Wouldn't Matter!
by
Bruce A. Howell

Another general conference global missions service had come and gone. The theme was "More." We asked men and women to give more of themselves; not merely their money. We needed more sacrifice and passion for the mission so we could reach more people! Like most global missions services at general conference, I walked away touched, stirred, challenged, and hopefully changed. I know that missionaries have sacrificed so much, yet they share the same response when attending such meetings. What is the reward of your great sacrifice?

Evangelist Billy Cole preached a message at School of Missions one year, "The Reward of Sacrifice." *(This sermon made it into his book* Teachings by Billy Cole.*) His text was 1 Samuel 6:7-14. Two cows were tied to a cart to carry the Ark of the Covenant. Their calves were kept at home. The two cows lowed as they went on their way. That was their initial sacrifice. Reaching their destination, the cart was destroyed; and the cows paid the ultimate sacrifice—their lives as a burnt offering. I remember Evangelist Cole saying, "The reward for sacrifice is another bigger sacrifice!" We are always called upon for more!*

Following is an excerpt from Melinda Poitras, one of our precious missionary kids:

"The book is American Literature. *It rests in the second drawer of my desk. It has been laughed at; highlighted; written in; and on one or more occasions, thrown across the room. I discovered Ben Hur and Moby Dick in this book. The Fireside Poets, the Knickerbocker writers, and the painters of the Hudson River School dwell in its pages. Rip Van Winkle sleeps there. Emily Dickinson lives her reclusive life there, and even Negro spirituals resound from its chapters. There are lives in this book and there are deaths in this book. It is one such death that leaves me sobbing into my notebook, frantically searching for tissues like the idiot I often am. The selection is 'Shadow of the Almighty.' The author is Elizabeth Elliot. The characters are real. The story is earth shaking in its simple truth.*

"Jim Elliot and his wife Elizabeth were missionaries in Ecuador. They were called to minister to the Auca Indians. ('That's nice,' you might say. 'So what?' you might ask.) Here's the thing. The Aucas were a bit . . . antisocial with the exception of one thing. They played a game with all men—white and Indians alike. We'll call it, 'You Come and We'll Kill You!' (The Aucas generally won this game, by the way.) Jim Elliot had, of course, heard of this game; but it didn't bother him that much. See, God made the players, and Jim knew that God could change the game—if He wanted.

"Jim and some other missionary friends hopped into Nate Saint's plane and began making 'deliveries' to the Aucas every week. They would fly above their camp shouting Aucan phrases like 'Trade you a lance for a machete' and 'We like you!' and dropping gifts to the ground. This went on for awhile until they decided that it was time to dive in and test the waters of their faith. Jim knew he might never come back, but he was 'willing to die if that's what God wants.' He sent his wife a message after arrival, telling her of the beach and closing with the information that they were leaving at that moment to go straight to the Aucan village. He did meet an Aucan after all. Jim Elliot fulfilled his life's goal and took an Aucan by the hand.

"Two days later, on Sunday, January 8, 1956, the men for whom Jim Elliot had prayed for six years killed him and his four companions.

"The faith in that story is beautiful. I've heard this Jim Elliot quote all my life: 'He is no fool who gives what he cannot keep to gain what he cannot lose.' The power in that sentence is heart wrenching. And as I read it, I realize it is not his death that is making me cry. It is the knowledge that if I could live like that, really live like that, death wouldn't matter!" (Melinda Poitras)

Elizabeth Elliot in *Through Gates of Splendor* said, "Letters from many countries have told of God's dealings with hundreds of men and women, through the examples of five who believed literally that 'the world passeth away, and the lust thereof: but he that doeth the will of God abideth forever.'"

A. W. Tozer in *The Pursuit of God* said, "We are often hindered from giving up our treasures to the Lord out of fear for their safety. This is especially true when our treasures are loved ones, relatives, and friends. But we need have no such fears. Our Lord came not to destroy but to save. Everything is safe which we commit to Him."

"Not my will, but thine, be done!" (Luke 22:42). Alan Redpath said, "Don't expect God to reveal His will for you next week until you practice it for today."

Roy Lessin in *"As Unto Me"* said, "There may be times when you do your very best but still see your labors fail. You may even sacrifice time or money to help someone and receive no words of appreciation. Do it anyway, as unto me, for I am your reward."

Consider the story of the Good Samaritan (Luke 10:30-37). Jim George in *God's Man of Influence* suggests five areas of sacrificial service.

- ▲ Sacrifice of time (He stopped and helped the wounded man.)
- ▲ Sacrifice of resources (He gave his bandage and dressing for the wounds.)
- ▲ Sacrifice of personal transportation (He carried the man to the inn.)
- ▲ Sacrifice of life (He personally took care of the man.)
- ▲ Sacrifice of money (He gave money and promised to pay for the wounded man's continued care.)

He closes his study on sacrifice by saying, "The greater the level of your service to others, the greater the level of your influence on others."

"If you have men who will only come if they know there is a good road, I don't want them. I want men who will come if there is no road at all." (David Livingstone)

"Ministry that costs nothing accomplishes nothing. If the minister's life is without a measure of pain and sacrifice, his ministry will be without blessing." (Warren and David Wiersbe)

Never Count the Cost
by
Bruce A. Howell

Leonard Ravenhill in Meat for Men wrote, "Recently, we visited an elaborate and opulent temple in the Far East. This experience reminded me of one Christian visitor who, overwhelmed with the ornate place and its static wealth, asked a heathen worshipper, 'What is the actual cost of erecting a temple like this?' The startled devotee replied in pained surprise, 'What is the cost? This temple is for our god, and for him we never count the cost.'"

Ravenhill then quoted this ancient prayer:

Teach us, good Lord,
To serve Thee more faithfully;
To give and not to count the cost;
To fight and not to heed the wounds;
To toil and not to seek for rest;
To labor and not to ask for any reward
Save that of knowing that we do Thy will.

As I scan the list of heroes of faith in Hebrews 11, I notice these men and women of vision had one thing in common. When it came to serving their God, they never counted the cost. They willingly gave all. It's been years since I've heard that little song, "Take it all. . . . What this world can offer me, take it all. For one hundred years from now, it won't matter anyhow." Oh, for a resurgence of that attitude!

How much is biblically expected when it comes to contributing to the kingdom of heaven; making a kingdom investment? The answer contains three simple letters—ALL.

"Again, the kingdom of heaven is like unto treasure hid in a field; the which when a man hath found, he . . . selleth all that he hath, and buyeth that field. Again, the kingdom of heaven is like unto a merchant man, seeking goodly pearls: Who, when he had found one pearl of great price, went and sold all that he had, and bought it" (Matthew 13:44-46).

Living a Warfare Lifestyle
by
Bruce A. Howell

The Bible is about war. The battle, between good and evil, begins in the first pages of Genesis and concludes in the battlefield of the final pages of Revelation. The victor is already determined. Yet, the war is tough, protracted, and bloody. Hanging in the balance are lost souls—men and women; boys and girls. Global evangelism is constant combat in spiritual warfare.

John Piper admonishes us to live a war-time lifestyle. This means we intentionally invest our resources of time, talent, and finances in the task of world evangelism. We need to be proactive, rather than reactive.

Christians with a warfare lifestyle are not only interested in being added to the Kingdom, they are focused on advancing the kingdom. They are Kingdom-minded. They refuse to keep silent. They realize it isn't enough to be blessed; they know they are blessed to be a blessing. They have found something they love so much, from Someone that loves them so much, that they are willing to live in reckless abandon to the great commission of pleasing Him.

There is a huge difference between a warfare lifestyle and a peace-time mindset. Drifting into a peace-time mentality is when we start feeling at "home" in this world, and look at luxuries as needs. We forget the urgency of rescuing the battle-scarred and lost; those that are perishing.

Some of us are old enough to remember the sacrifices made during World War II. The whole country changed its priorities. Everyone tried to help; both those at home and abroad. Raw materials were needed for the wartime effort so rationing took place.

items were restricted. Necessities became scarce. Everyone sacrificed. No one was exempt. Everyone cut back and reprioritized. There was a sense of commonality. We were all in the war together; those that went, and those that stayed. People wondered, "What can be done to advance the cause and ensure victory?" Everyone answered the call for personal involvement.

The strength of the church is not measured by those who sit protected on padded pews, but those soldiers that are sent forth to wage war. They march to the orders of their Commander-in-Chief, stay faithful to His plan of search and rescue; and never retreat. They charge forward in fulfillment of the Great Commission. Such warriors agree with the words of J. Hudson Taylor, "The Great Commission is not an option to be considered; it is a command to be obeyed." Missions is—and must always be—the battle cry of every born-again believer.

Thank God for our missionaries and national ministers on the frontlines gaining monumental territories and strategic victories. They are truly advancing the kingdom and making an eternal impact on their world. But, that is not enough. Must they go alone? All need to be enlisted in the battle. That, by the way, includes you and does not exclude me.

We can pray: "Ask of me, and I shall give thee the heathen for thine inheritance, and the uttermost parts of the earth for thy possession" (Psalms 2:8). I like how The Message paraphrases it, "What do you want? Name it: Nations as a present? continents as a prize?" My response is a resounding "Yes," to both questions. God literally wants to put nations within our grasp. He is doing it now. It starts with prayer. It is fueled by giving. It presses forward through going.

The Christian life hasn't changed. There is still a raging battle to be fought. We press forward knowing that one day we can testify, with Paul, "I have fought the good fight, I have finished the course. I have kept the faith" (2 Timothy 4:7).

We should not look at life casually. We cannot live each day carelessly. We need to recognize that there is a cause. Otherwise, there will be numerous spiritual casualties. Remember, what David said, as he contemplated the battle with Goliath, "Is there not a cause?" (1 Samuel 17:29). There certainly is. Unlike, David and Goliath, this battle cannot be fought and won alone. We need the united efforts of the entire church. It is time to live a warfare lifestyle. Can we sign you up for battle?

Submission

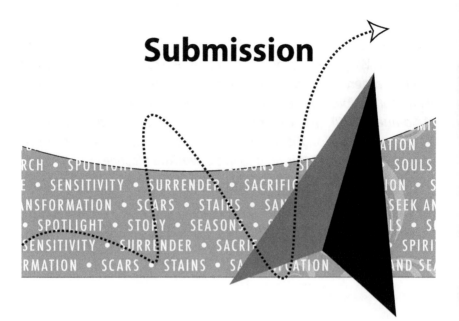

Submission is willingly giving up your own desires in favor of God's desires. A prerequisite to knowing the will of God is the willingness to submit and obey. Jesus asked, "Why do you call me, 'Lord, Lord,' and do not what I say?" (Luke 6:46, New International Version).

"His mother saith unto the servants, Whatsoever he saith unto you, do it" (John 2:5).

It is one thing to know. It is quite another to do. Are you teachable? Will you follow God's will once you know it?

"The Lord is my shepherd; I shall not want. He maketh me to lie down in green pastures: he leadeth me beside the still waters. He restoreth my soul: he leadeth me in the paths of righteousness for his name's sake" (Psalms 23:1-3).

Remember the old song by E. W. Brandy: "Where He leads me, I will follow. I'll go with Him, with Him all the way."

"Show me the way I should go; for to you I lift up my soul. . . . Teach me to do your will, for you are my God; may your good Spirit lead me on level ground" (Psalms 143:8, 10, NIV).

Submission is the willingness to do things God's way. "Submit yourselves therefore to God. Resist the devil, and he will flee from you. Draw nigh unto God, and he will draw nigh to you. Cleanse your hands, ye sinners; and purify your hearts, ye double minded" (James 4:7-8).

Submission is manifested by an obedient and teachable spirit. "Trust in the LORD with all thine heart; and lean not unto thine understanding. In all your ways acknowledge him, and he shall direct thy paths" (Proverbs 3:5-6).

Adam and Eve failed to submit to God's Word. They did not believe that He meant what He said.

Submission is bringing yourself under the protection of another. That is a concept some seem to quickly forget or bypass. I shudder to hear someone express, "I will listen only to God. I do not have to listen to authority or anyone." So sad! So destructive!

Global Impact Is the Least We Can Do
by
Bruce A. Howell

I had the privilege of co-chairing the Executive Global Council with the former UPCI General Superintendent Kenneth Haney. He reminded us that we need to pay the price for revival. He called us back to the preaching and way of the cross. Self-denial is the way to the heart of this world. He told a story of a communist boy, standing on a street corner, wearing tattered clothes, propagating communism. Someone walked by and said, "You're paying a big price for communism!" The boy responded, "When you're changing the world, no cost is too great."

Superintendent Haney told us, "Don't live one more day without a dream." He asked that we adopt the attitude that each of *us has ten years. Imagine that at the end of that time the trumpet would sound. He asked, "How would we live? What would be our vision? What would we do?" He ended with a solemn thought, "The reality is that we may have less than ten years. Global impact is the least we can do!"*

Spiritual Transformation

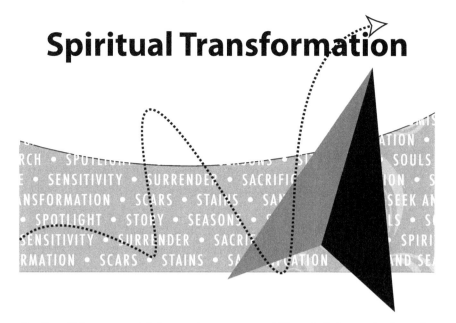

God's will begins with being born again. "The sinful mind is hostile to God. It does not submit to God's law, nor can it do so. Those controlled by the sinful nature cannot please God" (Romans 8:6-8, NIV). In Christ, we have become new creatures (II Corinthians 5:17); and as such, we are being transformed into the image of our Creator (Colossians 3:10). Since we refuse to be conformed to the pattern of the world or squeezed into its mold, we are able to sense the will of God (Romans 12:2). Doing what we ought to do (God's sovereign will) comes first. It is already revealed throughout Scripture. Then, as we digest the solid food of His Word, our powers of discernment are trained by constant practice so that we can discern good and evil (Hebrews 5:14). Then we can take part in what God plans to do in us and through us.

Romans 12:1-2 are vital verses in the process of spiritual transformation. They tell us how we can move from "My life is my own. I will do whatever I please" to "My life is not my own. It belongs to God. I will do what He pleases." That is where true commitment begins.

Ray Stedman in "Discovering the Will of God" stated that Romans 12:1-2 contains four points about commitment.

First of all, "present your bodies." When we move our bodies into action, we have really given ourselves. It is more than presenting the good intentions. Stedman said, "Our minds may be committed, our spirits may be available, but, yet, not our bodies. . . . The first test of your commitment to Christ is this: Is it active involvement?"

Second, Paul admonishes us to become "a living sacrifice." We die daily to the flesh. We pull ourselves onto the altar of sacrifice. It is not for a day. It is for as long as we are "living."

Third, we must be "holy and acceptable to God." Jesus needs to be living in us. The flesh cannot please God. It must be crucified. Stedman goes on to say, "God has put all that I am to death—my plans, my programs, my desires—all are tainted with self, and are worthless." This must be replaced with "Christ, who lives in me, to begin to work out His plans, His programs, His ideals, His desires."

Last, it is our "reasonable service." We yield to God what we were made to be, and do what we were made to do. It is only reasonable.

In doing those four things and refusing to conform to the thinking of the world, we are able to sense, prove, and discern the good, acceptable, and perfect will of God. God's will is "good." "All things work together for good, to those who love God, who are the called according to His purpose" (Romans 8:28). It is not always easy. It was not necessarily meant to be fun. However, it is always "good." As we walk on with God, we find it "acceptable," even when it includes trials, sufferings, and hardships. We also recognize it (usually in hindsight) as being "perfect." Given the opportunity, we would live it the same way again.

Scars

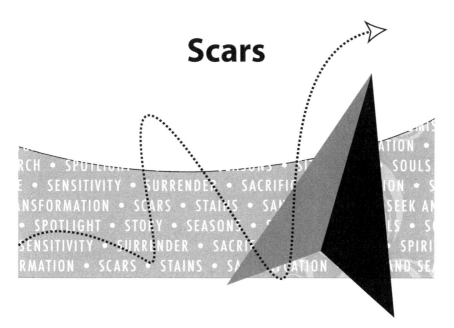

Being used of God does not mean we have to be perfect. Someone has said, "God never wastes a hurt!"

"Let the weak say, I am strong!" (Joel 3:10).

"From henceforth let no man trouble me: for I bear in my body the marks of the Lord Jesus" (Galatians 6:17).

Each ingredient of a cake is not necessarily good. But all the ingredients working together produce a good cake (Romans 8:28). Everyone passes through the School of Hard Knocks—of difficult life experiences. It breaks, shapes, and makes us. Someone once said, "He who bears no cross deserves no crown." No cross, no crown. No battle, no victory. Our experiences make us profitable to others and God's kingdom. One man referred to our role as "wounded healers." Because we have felt the sting of wounds, we are in the best position to adequately minister to others who are wounded and/or hurting.

Warren and David Wiersbe in *Ten Power Principles for Christian Service* said, "The nature of Christian ministry is such that it presents us with daily opportunities that can become either tests to build us up or temptations to tear us down." Life's experiences can make us better or bitter.

"And not only so, but we glory in tribulations also: knowing that tribulation worketh patience; And patience, experience; and experience, hope" (Romans 5:3-4). Be cautious when praying for patience. The Scripture makes it plain that suffering, tribulations, trials, and tests produce patience. However, they also lead to experience and that brings hope.

"Moreover [let us also be full of joy now!] let us exult and triumph in our troubles and rejoice in our sufferings, knowing that pressure and affliction and hardship produce patient and unswerving endurance. And endurance (fortitude) develops maturity of character (approved faith and tried integrity). And character [of this sort] produces [the habit of] joyful and confident hope of eternal salvation" (Romans 5:3-4, AMP).

Tim Hansel in *Holy Sweat* told of a revealing research done concerning 413 famous and gifted people. Two researchers spent years trying to discover the source of their greatness. The common thread that ran through most (392) of their lives was that they had to triumph over difficult obstacles in order to become who they were. Obstacles became opportunities.

Nancy Shirley in her lesson "Addicted to the Ministry" wonders what might have been said of Jesus in His day:

Heritage	Joseph isn't your father!
Birthplace	A barn.
Birth announcement	By shepherds, not too well known for their integrity in those days.
Name	One of the most common in the land.
Looks	No beauty in Him that we should desire Him.
Neighborhood	Can any good thing come out of Nazareth?
Wealth	A pair of turtle doves at His circumcision; a borrowed tomb at His death.
Status	Servant of all.
Possessions	Not a place to lay His head.

Goal in life	Born to die.
Temperament	A man of sorrows, acquainted with grief.
Popularity	Despised and rejected of men.
Companions	A friend of prostitutes and sinners.

Scars did not stop Jesus from effective ministry. Neither should you allow yours to hold you back. Scars can be stumbling blocks or stepping stones. Step into a bright future.

Stains

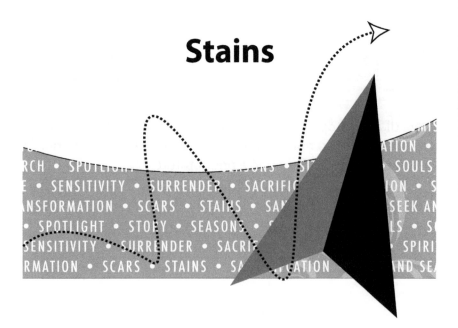

Stained Glass Window
by
Candra J. Poitras

Ever dropped something made of glass? Come on. In all truthfulness pretty much everyone has the typical glass-breaking-trauma story. Mine may or may not have something to do with the Rodenbush's butter dish…or I guess I should say, former butter dish. The bad thing about glass breaking is that you can't put it back the way it was. After you have shattered something on the kitchen floor, it isn't exactly possible to simply put it back together. Once broken, there is no going back.

Ever felt much like that broken glass? Lying on the floor; shattered in dozens of pieces. Unfixable. Permanently damaged. Past the point of hope. Perhaps you now feel as though you are broken into hundreds of tiny pieces and you will never be put back together into one whole piece again. The situation is a mission impossible; a dying cause. Or so you think. What if all your concepts are wrong? You see, for the most part, the breaking of glass is always viewed as a bad thing, when in reality it can be very good.

In the Middle Ages, a new art form became popular and has carried through even till today—the fine art of the stained glass window. I don't know how much you know about stained glass windows, but I googled them and everything, so I am now quite the expert. For all of you less informed in the art, stained glass windows start out as panes of glass that must be broken into pieces. Actually, more specifically, they aren't broken at all, but rather, cut to fit a specific design. The glass isn't stained, but painted in great detail by the master's hand.

"For I know the thoughts that I have towards you, saith the Lord, thoughts of peace, and not of evil, to give you an expected end" (Jeremiah 29:11). Before you were formed in your mother's womb, God had a specific plan for you. The blueprint is already made; the end of your story written. Now, here is the thing. What if all the things we have been through, all the trials, heartbreaks, failures, and disappointments, what if all the things that left you broken, what if they didn't leave you broken at all? Perhaps, it was the Lord cutting, shaping, and molding you to fit his master plan. What if the things that you thought left you broken, useless, and stained, were actually the Lord shaping and cutting you into the masterpiece He always intended you to be?

Romans 8: 28-30 says, "And we know that all things work together for good to them that love God, to them who are called according to his purpose. For whom he did foreknow, he also did predestinate to be conformed to the image of his Son, that he might be the firstborn amongst many brethren. Moreover whom he did predestinate, them he also called: and who he called, them he has also justified: and whom he justified, them he also glorified."

First of all, "all things work together for good to them that love God." I think a lot of the time we can interpret that incorrectly. It does not say that everything will always be good, that we won't have problems, or pain, or suffering. It says that if we love God and are called, He will take all of those things and use them for your good.

Secondly, "to them who are called according to His purpose." How many of you feel like God has placed a calling on your life? Ever feel like you have been called and things have gone on, and mistakes have been made, and you feel disqualified a bit from your calling? Well, that isn't what my Bible says. My Bible says that as long as you love the Lord and are called, He had a plan for you before you were even born. He already knew the end of you story as well as the beginning and middle. And He justified your past. Therefore, he knew long before you were born how things were going to turn out and He has already taken care of it.

The last component of a stained glass window is the glue or mortar that puts all the pieces back. It comes along and fills in all the cracks. It is the finishing; the thing that holds our world together. Our strength when we are weak, our comfort when we are weary, our help in time of need, He is the Alpha and Omega, the Beginning and the end. He is Daystar, Prince of Peace, Everlasting Wonder, Great I Am, and Counselor. His name is Jesus; the glue that completes the puzzle of His master plan for your life. Without the last component, you can do nothing. If you step out of His will and purpose, you become nothing more than little broken pieces of glass. His master plan for your life has to contain both you and Him. Without both, the plan cannot succeed.

The pain may be great, though the process may not be pleasant, but if you will just submit yourself to His master plan and allow Him to be the glue that holds your world together, the end result may just stun the world with its beauty. And don't you find it interesting that the most intricate stained glass windows are the ones that must be broken/cut the most? Surrender to His plan, follow His will, stick to Jesus in the process, and know that the end result is going to be simply beautiful. Allow Jesus to fill in the cracks of your life and shape you into His masterpiece.

Sanctification

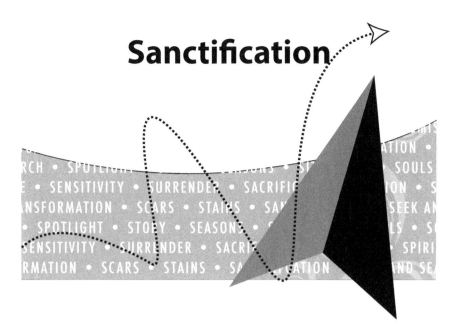

"For this is the will of God, even your sanctification, that ye should abstain from fornication: that everyone of you should know how to possess his vessel in sanctification and honour; not in lust of concupiscence, even as the Gentiles which know not God" (I Thessalonians 4:3-5).

Sanctification is "the state of being set apart for a purpose, separated unto God." Too often we connect the will of God with:

- ▲ Location: Where should I go?
- ▲ Vocation: What should I do?

But the most important question is "What should I be?" God is interested in our character—in what we are becoming. It is pivotal for each of us to live a life of holiness and purity, abstaining from sin. John Wesley once wrote to his mother, Susanna, and asked for a list of sins to avoid. She wisely responded, "Whatever weakens your reason, whatever impairs the tenderness of your conscience, whatever obscures your sense of God, whatever increases the authority of your body over your mind, whatever takes away from your relish for spiritual things, that to you is sin, no matter how innocent it is in itself."

"'Your task . . . to build a better world,' God said. I answered, 'How? The world is such a large, vast place, and there's nothing I can do.' But God in all His wisdom said, 'Just build a better you.'" (Author Unknown)

Seek and Search

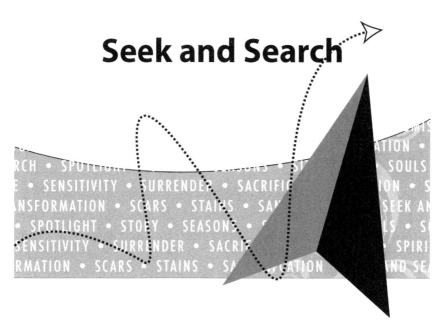

Seek the lost, "For the Son of man is come to seek and to save that which was lost" (Luke 19:10).

The "Wait" of the Harvest
by
Bruce A. Howell

News flash! Something incredible has taken place on earth. Population has surpassed 6.4 billion. Our world now boasts of 440 mega cities with more than one million inhabitants each. What an awesome opportunity! With such impressive prospects, why am I experiencing sleepless nights? Why this nervous awareness that the waiting harvest is slipping through our hands? Why the haunting dreams of untouched cities? Why do images of lost souls pass through my mind like PowerPoint presentations?

The weight of the world hovers over me, inescapable every minute of my day. I can't get away from it! I am consumed with reaching the world. This is the day of the church. God wants to give us revival that we cannot imagine. But He expects wise and proper stewardship of our time, talent, and treasure. We need more workers in the field so we can facilitate the end-time outpouring the Lord has promised.

What's the big deal? Jesus identified it. There is a gigantic crop, but few reapers (Luke 10:2). No workers. No reaped harvest. It's as simple as that! The solution is as obvious. We need more people to carry the truth to the waiting billions. Will you carry the weight of the harvest!

"For God so loved the world, that he gave his only begotten Son, that whosoever believeth in him should not perish, but have everlasting life" (John 3:16). I once tried to teach this verse to my little girl. She kept getting hung up on "begotten." She would say, "For God so loved the world, that he gave his only *forgotten* Son." Really, it was good theology.

God loved us so much that He forgot Himself, became flesh, and came and dwelt among us (John 1:1-14). Jesus paid the price on Calvary for our redemption. "For God bought you with a high price" (I Corinthians 6:20, NLT). The songwriter said, "He paid a debt He did not owe. I owed a debt I could not pay. I needed someone to wash my sins away" (Ellis J. Crum). If God was willing to pay such an enormous cost, imagine how valuable a lost soul must be in His sight.

Evangelism is our main concern. Proclaim the gospel. Win the lost to Christ. Bringing someone to Him requires time, effort, and financial investment. Is it worth it? Jesus thought so. Luke 15 could be titled "The Lost Chapter." Notice it follows the account of "The God of the Full House." "And the lord said unto the servant, Go out into the highways and hedges, and compel them, to come in that my house may be filled" (Luke 14:23).

Luke 15 tells three short stories of things lost. The discerning reader will even find a fourth. The chart that follows reveals things lost and the value they represented.

Things Lost	Things Represented
Lost lamb	Livelihood
Lost coin	Life's savings
Lost son	A family's investment in a life

Jesus gave these parables in response to sharp criticism from the scribes and Pharisees. They were shocked that Jesus spent so much time with sinners and even ate with them. They gave Him a tough time. They reasoned, "You can tell the character of a man by looking at the company he keeps!" "You show me your friends, and I'll show you what type of person you are." Luke 15 highlights our invitation to follow the Master's example in aggressively seeking for the lost and to rejoice as sinners are reached. The religious leaders had missed the point because of their maintenance mindset.

Jesus came to save sinners. He recognized their soul value and sought to reclaim them for the kingdom. They embodied His purpose in dropping into our world. He came for those that needed help.

Jesus set His listeners up. "Wouldn't you leave . . . and *go* after the lost one *until* you found it?" (Luke 15:4, *The Message*, Emphasis the Author's). The answer was obvious to the spectators. In each of the three stories someone searched non-stop for the lost or watched, waited, or longed for something. We give up too easily. God, give us a spirit of endurance and diligence. Some of us are naïve enough to think that the lost should find their own way into the church. That has never been the biblical imperative. We are repeatedly admonished to "go!"

Each of the three stories has the following in common:

- ▲ Something lost.
- ▲ Something sought or longed for.
- ▲ Something found.
- ▲ Something celebrated.

Dr. Neil Chadwick in his sermon "Lost and Found" said, "The value of a particular item can be determined according to the amount of effort invested in finding it, if and when it becomes lost." The emphasis in each story is not on the time it takes to find the lost, but on the value of it.

Just like the shepherd going out into the night searching for the lost sheep, Jesus vigorously and tirelessly seeks lost souls. He expects more than our silent witness.

The lady searching thoroughly for her lost coin reminds us that we are looking for something valuable and costly. She used what she had. We often think we need special equipment or resources to be evangelistic. Just use what you have. The woman took a candle, providing light, to increase her chances of seeing. She also used her broom to carefully sweep the vicinity. She continued to "seek diligently" until she found her valued possession (Luke 15:8).

The third story refers to the prodigal son. The NIV is more specific when it calls him the "lost son." He takes his inheritance, spends it on worldly living, comes to himself, and returns home. In him we clearly see the basic state of mankind—rebellious and disobedient. "Father, I have sinned against both heaven and you, and I am no longer worthy of being called your son" (Luke 15:18-19, NIV). The lost son thought his value had decreased because of his sinful actions.

The loving father is God. He is depicted as waiting, watching, running, embracing, kissing, and rejoicing. Christianity is the only world religion that has such a loving Father who enthusiastically seeks men. The elder brother, out of touch with his father's heartbeat, is compared to the Pharisees. His father reasoned, "But it was fitting to make merry, to revel and feast and rejoice, for this brother of yours was dead and is alive again! He was lost and is found!" (Luke 15:32, AMP). We can hear the Father's heart beating throughout Scripture as we read about Him saving lost souls. He is moved to compassion as He looks over a gone-astray world. Evangelism is the heartbeat of God. His desire is that none of His children be lost.

"Rejoice with me . . . I tell you, there is rejoicing in the presence of the angels of God over one sinner who repents" (Luke 15:9-10, NIV). Jesus did not specifically say angels are partying, but that there is rejoicing "in the presence of the angels." Conceivably, we have read these verses and imagined the angels breaking into a praise dance. Maybe they do. If the angels are not the ones rejoicing, who is? It is our caring, heavenly Father. Add to this the possibility of a wider crowd—the saints that have gone before and the great cloud of witnesses (Hebrews 12:1). One thing for sure, God celebrates when a lost soul repents—turning from the wrong path to the right one. And anything that makes God happy should make us happy too.

Every service should be a celebration when we see someone repent, baptized in Jesus' name, and/or filled with the Holy Ghost. Heaven is standing by. God is ready for a divine party. All that is needed is for a lost soul to be found.

Below is a summary of the conditions found in each narrative:

Subject	Path to Being Lost	Conditions
Sheep	Lost through ignorance	Lost and knew it was lost; did not know its way home.
Coin	Lost through carelessness or neglect of others	Lost, but did not know it was lost; did not know its way home.
Son	Lost through his own willfulness	Lost, and knew he was lost; knew his way home.

Reading through Luke 15 have you determined how you can fit into the stories?

- ▲ Become the shepherd searching for the frightened lost lamb.
- ▲ Become the woman, lighting the candle of the gospel, searching for the coin insignificant to others.

▲ Become like the loving father anxiously praying, waiting, and watching for the lost son's return home. Get in touch with your Dad's heartbeat!

Vance Havner wrote of the Titanic that sank in 1912. (Remember, it was reputed to be unsinkable.) "The only thing it ever did was sink." Departing from England it had all sorts of passengers aboard. There were millionaires, celebrities, middle-income earners, and even poor folks. There were people from all walks of life. But a few hours after the historical disaster, when they published a list in New York, it carried only two categories—lost and saved. In the end all distinctions are set aside. It all comes down to lost or saved—lost or found.

Seek God's will. The principle in God's Word is, "If you don't seek, you won't find." "Ask, and it shall be given you; seek, and ye shall find; knock, and it shall be opened unto you: for every one that asketh receiveth; and he that seeketh findeth; and to him that knocketh it shall be opened" (Matthew 7:7-8).

"But seek ye first the kingdom of God, and his righteousness; and all these things shall be added unto you" (Matthew 6:33).

The Fire Still Falls
by
Melinda Poitras

We say, "People don't want God.
People don't care.
We try and we try;
They don't notice we're there!"

We stand fast in God's compassion,
And the love He came to prove;
Yet fall short of believing
That He can still move.

Arise, oh believer!
Lift up your head.
The voice of truth calls you.
God is not dead!

People are searching;
Won't you show the way?
Remember to love them;
Remember to pray.

For across the great distance
God still softly calls.
The war is still raging.
The fire still falls.

Spotlight

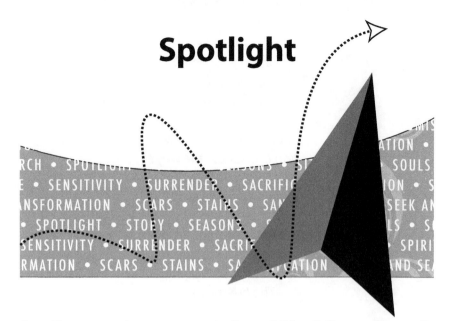

Jim Sleeva, an instructor at Indiana Bible College often tells students, "Exposure breeds a burden." A young person on the Next Step program in the Baltic Republics expressed, "My calling is reinforced when missionaries visit our church." Obviously this is one of the many reasons for face-to-face contact with missionaries as they travel on deputation.

Seeing Challenges, Solutions, and Horizons
by
Bruce A. Howell

Seems almost everyone is looking for a hero. Some wildly imagine super heroes, equipped with mega-powers, dressed in capes and tights, battling the forces of good and evil, only brought down by kryptonite or some other outlandish phenomena. Others celebrate and idolize sports heroes struggling to make yard-line progress, chasing or catching pigskin, pursued by hefty opponents. They relish the adrenalin rush of victory and shrink under the drain of defeat. In missions we honor and appreciate spiritual heroes. By faith they walk into the world of the unknown—unknown languages, unknown cultures, unknown resources, and unknown circumstances. They do not walk by sight. They walk by promise. "I have set before you an open door" (Revelation 3:8). "Every place that the sole of your feet will tread upon, I have given to you" (Joshua 1:3, English Standard Version). "I will be with you!"

Admittedly, I wasn't feeling I fit into any category of heroes the early morning I rolled out of bed in Manila, Philippines. Yes, I jubilated in the fiftieth year of the United Pentecostal Church in these islands. I praised God for His faithfulness and supernatural empowerment. I nostalgically recalled the sacrifices of multiple missionaries and hundreds of Filipino leaders who had provided the nourishment of blood, sweat, and tears that ensured the progress of the church to this stage. Yet, my mind was tortured by the millions in Manila who still needed truth, the dozens of countries waiting for the gospel light, and the struggles of circumstances faced by several of our missionary front liners.

I needed to get out for a bit of exercise. I considered jogging, but lacked the zeal or the needed strength and speed. A walk would suffice. I launched into Ayala Street—Manila's Wall Street equivalent. I admired the stunning structures, awed by how they painted such a dramatic contrast to the ghetto areas. Walking briskly through a tunnel, I noticed a bank sign. The words captivated me: **"See challenges, not barriers; see solutions, not differences; and see horizons, not borders."** I stood gazing at the sign quietly memorizing the motto. People detoured around me, giving me a suspicious glance. I had found a gem, a bit of signboard theology. It was amazing, a nugget for a sermon by merely paying attention. I knew I had to preach that line, and since then, I have done so several times. This treasured phrase suitably depicts the heroes of global missions—our veterans.

My heart makes a slow journey into my throat, and tears ripple down my cheeks, as I survey the sacrifices missionaries have made and are making to bring us to where we are. Daniel Scott said it right: our veteran missionaries are "like seeds, which, planted in the earth, burst forth to yield much fruit." How do you count from one to nearly two million constituents? One soul at a time! Sacrifice equals *souls gained. It began when our organization saw their mission as taking "the whole gospel to the whole world." Missionaries stepped forward armed with vision. They saw challenges, not barriers. They saw solutions, not differences. They envisioned horizons, not borders.*

Here is a sampling of how the overseas church was planted in the over six decades that have brought us to modern missions in the United Pentecostal Church International:

- *I've stood beside the grave where missionary parents buried their beloved daughter killed in an accidental shooting.*

- *I've journeyed to areas where missionaries started their labors in a leprosy colony or stood on street corners holding an English tract asking, "Can you read this?"*

- *I've visited three nations where missionaries lost their lives in automobile accidents.*

- *I've visited churches destroyed by civil war and wept as I walked with missionary giants, who with their saints, stood strong through it all.*

- *I've stood helplessly by the caskets of veteran missionaries who came home from their fields, stricken in health, and died months or a few short years later.*

- *I've been there, trying to get the release of a missionary who died on the foreign field, so the body could be shipped home to a waiting family.*

- *I've hugged the necks of missionaries as they sent their kids from their homes to North America.*

- *I've written countless e mails, prayed numerous prayers, to and for faithful missionaries going through struggles.*

- *I've read of a missionary hero that died of a stroke, at the age of eighty-three, and was buried on the field; of a husband who built a wooden casket for his late wife; and of a small son buried overseas.*

- *I've read about a missionary lady who dreaming of winning the world was dead within six months of arriving on location, and of her missionary colleague who buried her.*

- *I'm amazed at the sacrifice of a missionary, pioneering works in several nations, preaching one last message, collapsing into a coma and dying, then buried on his field.*

- *I've wondered how strong I would be … lost in the fog in a little plane or in a plane wreck where missionaries miraculously walked away.*

- *I'm awed by the missionary lifers who waited seventeen long years for registration and resident permits in the country where they longed to go.*

- *I'm overwhelmed with the courage of a missionary lady who was the last foreigner to board a plane after a coup d'état.*

- *I've daydreamed of how I would have stood or withstood being in a concentration camp for seven months, or how I would have managed a funeral a day after a plane crashed into the mighty Amazon claiming one of my missionaries and nationals. In the four years after that crash over four thousand were baptized in Jesus' name. Multitudes still gather on the beach close to the crash site for regular baptismal services. Entire villages in that area are United Pentecostal.*

In each case of sacrifice, revival has ensued; and the church has surged forth in growth. Every advancement was a result of seeing possibilities in impossibilities. Each saw challenges, not barriers; solutions, not differences; and horizons, not borders. Each surrendered a life, went to a land, and left a legacy.

Missionary Cathy Lynn Killoren
She Was in the Soul-saving Business
by
Bruce A. Howell

Cathy Lynn Killoren was born April 29, 1955. She was converted in her last year of high school, graduated from Jackson College of Ministries in 1976, went to El Salvador on the Associates in Missions program in 1989, and received missionary appointment in 1995. She labored devotedly in this tiny revival nation even though she experienced health setbacks that, despite excellent medical care, culminated in her passing. Her faithfulness under difficult circumstances is a testimony to all. Her prayer was if God did not see fit to restore her health that He should take her. God saw best to call her to rest.

"And I heard a voice from heaven saying unto me, Write, Blessed are the dead which die in the Lord from henceforth: Yea, saith the Spirit, that they may rest from their labours; and their works do follow them" (Revelation 14:13).

On behalf of the leadership, pastors, and over 100,000 constituents in the United Pentecostal Church of El Salvador, I mention these words concerning our departed, much loved, and long-to-be-remembered Cathy Killoren: "For God is not unrighteous to forget or overlook your labor and the love which you have shown for His name's sake in ministering to the needs of the saints" (Hebrews 6:10, AMP). Because of Cathy's commitment, burden, love, and ministry, one day multiplied thousands of Salvadorians will rejoice and reunite with her in Heaven.

Cathy was respectfully known from the president's office to the humblest and poorest areas in this Central American nation. She loved to work with children in orphanages, encourage the ladies, and assist in preaching points. She was instrumental in the successful ministry of the mobile medical clinic. As a result, a church was established in San Juan La Ceiba. Thousands of Bible studies were taught as people awaited treatment.

Cathy's life reminds me of the initial thinking of a group, started over three hundred years ago, concerned with lives lost in the Atlantic Ocean within a mile from land. This little cluster couldn't stand to think of people going down so close to their shores, so they went into the lifesaving business. They built little huts of refuge along the shoreline. Their motto was, "You have to go out, but you don't have to come back!" They took their task seriously and risked all because they prized human life. Over time the US Coast Guard took over the job and adopted the same values. Souls are lost on the seas and in the storms of life. Our commission has not altered. Cathy went out, realizing that she did not have to come back. She was in the soul-saving business!

Story

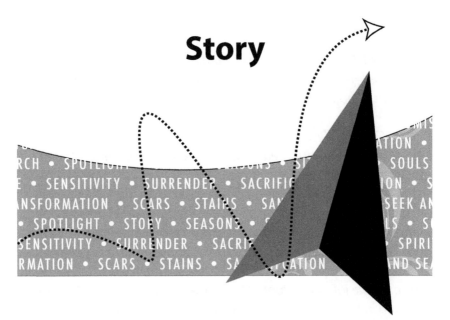

Everyone has a call story. Gordon MacDonald in *God's Calling Plan* said, "A 'call story' is a history of whispering words and events that capture the soul and make us aware God is speaking."

Some call stories are dramatic. Others are audible. Some are like continual dropping until you respond, "Okay, Lord!" David Livingstone never got away from "I have sometimes seen in the morning sun the smoke of a thousand villages where no missionary has ever been." The idea kept coming back.

Crown Financial Ministries, in "Knowing God's Will" said, "God doesn't use burning bushes much anymore to communicate with His people, but He does communicate through burning hearts—hearts that are in tune to His Word and hearts that love and worship their Lord Jesus Christ."

Missionary James Burton,
Our Faithful Friend
by
Bruce A. Howell

Four generations of Burtons have either lived or ministered on Venezuelan soil. Other members of the family have served God in the homeland. They knew James Burton as husband, father, and grandfather. I knew him as a dear friend. When I was a young missionary in El Salvador, Venezuela was one of the first countries outside of Central America that I visited. When he was field superintendent, Missionary Burton invited me there several times, and I was privileged to have him with us in El Salvador. He was quiet, possessed a peaceful spirit; was always cheerful, smiling, and kind. When encountering James Burton, one quickly felt overshadowed in the presence of a gentle giant.

Faithful: James Burton sensed the call to distant South America when he was sixteen years of age. He and his wife attended Bible school, developed their ministries, and were appointed as global missionaries in 1961. A year later they boarded a boat and headed for Venezuela, never once looking back, always faithful to the call. Upon arrival at their new ministerial home, they found three small churches and one preaching point. The foundation had been faithfully laid by others, and the Burtons immediately started to build on it.

In those days of my "youth meetings," I quickly saw that Venezuela was one of the best kept secrets of the UPCI. Missionary Burton was a strong administrator, dedicated to establishing a Bible school. The work was formed through teaching. The UPC in that nation became well organized and strong in the Apostolic doctrine. The Venezuelan UPC can count over 180,000 constituents, over 800 churches and preaching points, and over 1,000 active ministers of the gospel.

In 2007 we celebrated fifty years of the UPC reaching and winning lost souls in Venezuela. Founding missionaries Lewis Morley, Ernesto Martinez, and James Burton along with their families were honored. I was awed to look out over the 20,000 plus Venezuelans in attendance. Regional Director Darry Crossley later reported, "It was an amazing sight—the floor of the arena was packed with people standing for over three hours! The crowds in the bleachers had to be told to quit jumping for fear the whole structure would collapse!"

When James Burton sensed it was God's direction to turn the church over to national leadership, he left behind one of the strongest churches we have in the world. Building that church wasn't always easy. In fact, reaching souls and a nation is never easy. It is accomplished through faith and through faithful men and women. The church in Venezuela continues to thrive, growing rapidly each year, and is our largest work in South America.

Twenty-seven years after the Burtons arrived in Venezuela, the government took special notice of James Burton's faithfulness to their nation. A declaration was made; and the president presented him with a beautiful silver medal, the second highest award given for outstanding achievement. No Protestant missionary had ever before been honored for laboring among the Venezuelans.

Two years later James Burton accepted the challenge of becoming the regional field supervisor (now identified as regional director) of South America. For six years he faithfully executed his duties in this responsibility and provided leadership and encouragement to both missionaries and national leaders throughout South America. When many would have been happy to retire, the Burtons stepped out of being the regional director and into a new role as missionaries to Uruguay. He served until his health would allow him to serve no longer, and they returned to North America. The Burtons had served under appointment for thirty-eight years.

Not only will Missionary James Burton hear his Master pronounce, "Well done, good and faithful servant," he will receive the crown of life. Venezuela honored this faithful man with a silver medal and a declaration, but Heaven holds greater commendations. This man faithfully gave his life, went to a land, and left an undying legacy. The race has been run. The victory has been won. The champion, our faithful friend, has gone home.

Put Your Heart into It!
by
Bruce A. Howell

Put your heart into it! That, in a nutshell, summarizes the attitude I have concerning my work and ministry. I wholeheartedly want to give it my best shot. I don't ever want to lose heart, nor become faint-hearted, half-hearted, or cold-hearted about our lost world. I will either be whole-hearted or go into prayer and fasting until I have a change of heart.

There is an old chorus that adequately portrays the type of heart we should have when it comes to reaching souls:

> Take it all. Take it all.
> What this world can offer me, take it all.
> For one hundred years from now, it won't matter anyhow.
> What this world can offer me, take it all.
> (Author Unknown)

In global missions we often promote faith promise. It involves two parts: faith-giving and faith-going. John Leaman has often said, "Some give by going. Others go by giving. Without both there are no missions." We give and go because there is a big harvest, a gigantic need.

How much should one give to missions? In one developing country when settling the amount to be paid for services rendered, they are told, "Give whatever your heart tells you. Give from your heart." Faith promise and Partners-in-Missions is just that . . . **heart-giving**. God's Word agrees. "Each man should give what he has decided in his heart to give" (II Corinthians 9:7, NIV). Or as the Amplified Bible puts it: "Let each one [give] as he has made up his own mind and purposed in his heart, not reluctantly or sorrowfully or under compulsion, for God loves (He takes pleasure in, prizes above other things, and is unwilling to abandon or to do without) a cheerful (joyous, 'prompt to do it') giver [whose heart is in his giving]" (II Corinthians 9:7).

We can do more, and do better, as we put our heart into it.

Our faithful missionaries go across North America presenting their burden nightly for an average of thirteen months or more. What is their message? It's simple. The task cannot be accomplished alone. The missionary is saying, "For me to accomplish the call, I need you. For you to accomplish the call, you need me. I will sacrifice by going if you will sacrifice by giving." It is a partnership made up of faith-giving and faith-going.

My heart is full of admiration and thankfulness for thousands of missionaries, AIMers, and ministers who pour their hearts into God's kingdom around the globe. Else Lund served as a missionary for over forty-two years. She wrote, "These have been the happiest years of my life. If it were possible I would be happy to do it over and over again, except the part when I broke my hip." She went to West Africa when the only other mission work on the continent was in South Africa. She put her heart into the cause and never looked back. Literally over a thousand preachers have been trained by her.

Else Lund continues, "We have been lost in the fog in our UPC mission plane . . . and a couple of years later had a plane wreck on the way to the mission airstrip at Bomi Hills. . . . The plane was totaled, but we all walked away. . . . I have been in coups, attempted coups, an accident, a break-in, several attempted break-ins, civil war, had malaria untold times, and on and on."

As I worked on this article, I received word that 1,298 were filled with the Holy Ghost at the national conference in Madagascar. The Chris Richardson family had previously reported 1,493 receiving the Holy Ghost in regional conferences. Richardson *is a household name in UPCI missions and a very familiar one in Madagascar. Four generations have worked on that island and on the other islands of the Indian Ocean. Five sets of Richardsons have served or are serving under missionary appointment with the UPCI.*

The stories could go on and on of missionaries who tirelessly put their hearts into the mission. The results of their labors, and your support, speak loudly. We are reaching over 195 nations and have over 34,133 churches and preaching points overseas. In one year alone 104,906 were baptized in Jesus' name and 127,070 received the glorious baptism of the Holy Ghost.

Bill Bright said, "None of us has a long time here on planet earth. It's our split second in eternity when we have an opportunity to invest our lives to help fulfill what our Lord came into this world to do." That is an investment worth making, so put your heart into it!

Young David Livingstone listened intently to a seasoned missionary. "There is a vast plain to the north, where I have sometimes seen in the morning sun the smoke of a thousand villages where no missionary has ever been." Those words, "the smoke of a thousand villages," found a resting place deep in David's heart. He arrived in Cape Town at the age of twenty-seven and spent over half his life in Africa. He explored more than a third of African soil believing that he should keep on the move, instead of staying in one place preaching to a few people. He was convinced that the known world could be reached and that there was, and is, no such thing as a closed country to the gospel. He unreservedly proclaimed, "I will open a way to the interior or perish." The call of popularity and position did not soften his resolve: "I had rather be in the heart of Africa in the will of God than on the throne of England out of the will of God."

Late one night, Chuma and Susi, Livingstone's faithful African companions, entered his hut and found him kneeling at his bedside, his head buried in his hands on the pillow. Looking closer, they were shocked to find that he had died in prayer.

These African men carried David Livingstone's body for eleven months across Africa to the Indian Ocean. Months later his remains arrived in Europe and were buried in Westminster Abbey in London. However, his two friends buried his heart at the foot of a nearby tree in Zambia. They said his heart did not belong in England, for he had a heart for Africa. My heart leaps and tears spill just thinking about it.

You can count on me to put my heart into reaching my world. Can I count on you?

Paul in Acts 26:12-19, remembered his dramatic call story. Check it out! Will God have to knock you down before you can hear His voice?

Seasons

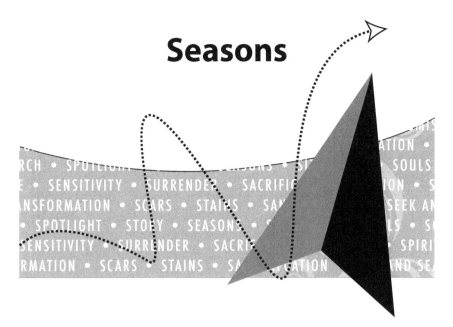

"There is a time for everything, and a season for every activity under heaven" (Ecclesiastes 3:1, NIV). God puts the right person, with the right ministry, in the right place, at the right time.

And Their Works Follow Them
by
Bruce A. Howell

Recently, I was in Ecuador for the second Spanish Summit. I heard Elias Limones speak about former missionary, Lucille Farmer. Elias was born in Ecuador where his father was a pastor. He remembers going with his dad to the airport to meet her. He had never seen a white lady with such blue eyes. He thought she was an angel. There was no money for a hotel, so the Limones family kept her in their home until she could find a place of her own. She stayed in a little back room with a concrete floor. She slept on a cot. She used dictionaries and sign language to communicate with the family.

Years later, when Elias was pastoring in the United States, he went to Oregon to visit her. She directed him to pull out a cardboard box of pictures kept in her humble room. They enjoyed looking through the pictures of his family from his childhood. Lucille Farmer was poor and didn't have much more than a cardboard box of memories. But, oh what rich treasures she left behind in Ecuador.

While in Quito, I saw over 1,500 ministers and wives representing Spanish-speaking nations. In one church in Quito, Leonardo Becerra pastors some 2,000 saints. How did this happen? Because a missionary was willing to make a great sacrifice. Sacrifice has eternal dividends and is a smart investment. I am reminded of this verse: "And I heard a voice from heaven saying unto me, Write, Blessed are the dead which die in the Lord from henceforth: Yea, saith the Spirit, that they may rest from their labours; and their works do follow them" (Revelation 14:13). The seeds planted by Missionary Farmer continue to bear fruit. Her works continue to follow her!

I recently visited Liberia where Pauline Gruse and others labored for many years. She even buried one of her missionary colleagues by herself.

Margaret Calhoun paid the ultimate sacrifice, yielding her life to the mighty Amazon River in a plane accident. She had worked side by side with the Bennie DeMerchant family (who arrived in Brazil in October 1965). Just in the Amazon drainage area are about 650 churches, over 500 ministers, and 45,000 constituents. In the city of Manaus alone are 125 churches. Along the Amazon, entire villages are part of the United Pentecostal Church. What happened? The missionaries' works have followed them! "Take no thought for your life, what ye shall eat, or what ye shall drink: nor yet for your body what ye shall put on. Is not life more than meat, and the body than raiment?" (Matthew 6:25).

In the midst of all the modern conveniences designed to ease living in the twenty-first century, God still calls men and women to sacrificially take the gospel to the ends of the earth. They are sacrificing today so that multiplied thousands can have a better tomorrow. People from every tribe, kindred, and tongue will be rejoicing around the throne in Heaven.

Max Lucado said, "It's what we do for Christ in the here and now that will make a difference in the then and there."

And their works do follow them!

Timing is important.
"When the fullness of the time was come"
"When the right time came" (NLT)
"When the proper time had fully come" (AMP)
"When the time had fully come" (Revised Standard Version)
"When the right time finally came" (Today's English Version)
(Galatians 4:4).

God takes us through various seasons in our lives.

Plowing	Preparing
Seedtime/planting	Sowing
Growth	Persevering
Harvest	Rejoicing

A call includes a time for preparation. "Praise be the name of God forever and ever; wisdom and power are his. He changes times and seasons" (Daniel 2:20-21, NIV). Do what God has already told you to do until He tells you to do something else.

Warren Wiersbe said, "God prepares the person for the work and the work for the person, and, if we permit Him, He brings them together in His providence." In *The Art & Craft of Biblical Preaching* Wiersbe also said, "He is always preparing us for what He has already prepared for us."

Rufus Parker in *A Reflection of the Man in the Mirror* stated, "The reason there are few laborers is not because God is not sending, but because we are not developing."

There are three types of time in the Bible:

Chronos	Chronological time; governed by the clock
Kairos	Right time or strategic time. This is time measured by special moments; God-moments.
Pleroo	Fullness of time

This can be aptly compared to life.

Chronos	Conception/pregnancy/development
Kairos	Labor
Pleroo	Birth/delivery

The same thing happens with the transition of the cocoon to a butterfly. We also could look at the life of Jesus:

Chronos	Birth, growth, and ministry
Kairos	The death, burial, and resurrection
Pleroo	The coming of the Holy Spirit at Pentecost

Myles Monroe asserted, "You only become what you are becoming right now." In his book *The Principles and Power of Vision*, he speaks of three stages of life:

Birth and dependency	Relying totally on outside help to survive
Independence	Capturing what we were born to do
Interdependence	Passing our dream and vision on to the next generation

Monroe, in *Seasons of Change*, said that seasons denote transition of time—the point of convergence when two seasons meet. Inherent in the seasons are these concepts:

▲ Change
▲ Transition

- ▲ Difference (replacing one season with another)
- ▲ Temporary conditions (Seasons are not permanent.)
- ▲ Time periods (Present conditions are subject to time.)

God bless you as you journey through the various seasons of change that come your way.

Situations

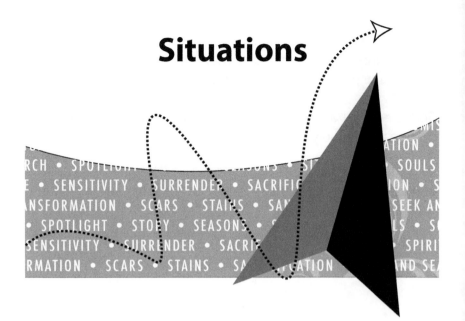

The experiences we go through are not accidents. They are appointments. Many times the will of God is sensed more effectively as hindsight rather than foresight. We look back over situations and see that God's hand and will were evident throughout the process. Let the will of God unfold for you. Be careful not to make life decisions when you are angry, confused, or frustrated. The same applies when you are in the valley. After you rest, climb. Make decisions on the peak, when you are on top of things emotionally, physically, and spiritually.

The story is told of the only survivor of a shipwreck who swam to a small island. He prayed that the Lord would send someone to rescue him. Every day he scanned the horizon to see if help was coming. It seemed hopeless, so he gathered palm fronds and scraps of wood to build a tiny hut.

One day as he returned to his hut after forging for food, he saw smoke rolling into the sky. He was shocked to find his little home in flames. The worst had happened. He was devastated. He screamed, "God, how could you allow this to happen to me?"

Early the next morning the sound of a boat awakened him. Help had arrived.

"How did you know that I was here?" asked the man.

His rescuers replied, "We saw your smoke signal."

God had answered—just not in the expected way. Like the smoke that rose from the little island, your prayers go up to the Lord.

Money is not an obstacle when a person is called. When we focus on His agenda, God assumes responsibility for our needs.

"If God gives such attention to the appearance of wildflowers—most of which are never even seen—don't you think he'll attend to you, take pride in you, do his best for you? What I'm trying to do here is to get you to relax, to not be so preoccupied with *getting,* so you can respond to God's *giving.* People who don't know God and the way he works fuss over these things, but you know both God and how he works. Steep your life in God-reality, God-initiative, God-provisions. Don't worry about missing out. You'll find all your everyday human concerns will be met" (Matthew 6:30-33, MSG).

Seer

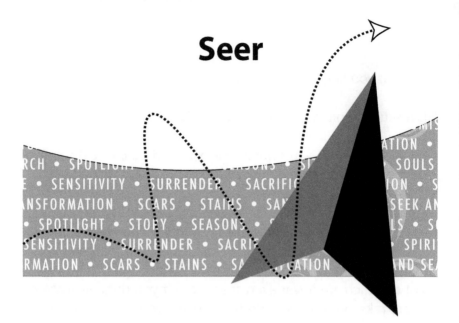

"Where there is no vision, the people perish: but he that keepeth the law, happy is he" (Proverbs 29:18).

View from the Summit
by
Bruce A. Howell

A legendary village chief lay dying. He called his three sons and told them, "I know I'll soon die. I must first choose one of you to be the next chief. I want you to climb the mountain and bring me something from there. Hurry!"

The three boys hurried off to the mountain. After a couple of days, the first returned and stood before the aged chief. "Father, I have climbed high on the mountain, and I have brought you a tree limb."

The chief asked him to wait for the return of the other two sons.

Several days passed before the second son returned. "Father, I have climbed high on the mountain and have gone above the tree line. I have brought you a rock."

After a long time, the third son returned. "Father," he began, "I have climbed high on the mountain. I have climbed to the top. From the summit I saw far into the distance. I saw the river flowing and smoke rising from distant huts. I saw the beauty of God's creation. However, I have nothing in my hand to bring you."

The old chief whispered, "You, my third son, will lead my people because even though you have nothing in your hand to bring me, you have something in your heart."

I can relate to that. God has placed a desire in my heart—and yours too—to reach our lost world. From the summit, we refocus our attention on the need, envisioning what can be done to make an eternal impact.

Recently, I looked carefully at my heart (and preached on the subject too). God does not usually work through us, unless He first works in us. I looked at dozens of heart types in God's Word. (I'll spare you the agony of dragging you through 830 references. I want to keep my readers!) The question came down to, "What type of heart do I have?"

The heart of the church is missions. It is reaching the lost. That is the view from the summit!

Vision casting experts tell us that one should be able to state his or her vision in twenty-one words or less. God does it in five. That's right, five. In the English language, the Bible reveals five words of vision that have affected over two thousand years of church planting and growth. These words announced the Lord's purpose in coming to the earth, His death on the cross, His powerful resurrection from the grave, and His ascension into Heaven. Because of five words of vision, He robed Himself in flesh.

Everything He did was focused on and measured through these

five words. Does this advance the cause—the vision?

False accusations did not stop Him. Betrayal did not stop Him. Beatings did not stop Him. A crown of thorns did not stop Him. The load of the cross did not stop Him. Calvary, the place of the skull, did not stop Him.

Why? Because He was driven by five words of vision. They were words of power, of potential, of purpose, of productivity. What were the words of vision? And what do they have to do with us? What do they have to do with the United Pentecostal Church International?

Our existence as a church is announced in those five words of vision. Our existence as a Christian is contingent upon them. Except for five words of vision we would have no need to remain on the earth. The same five words should be the reason for all that we do as a church. They are **"I will build my church"** (Matthew 16:18). That's five!

In every English translation of the Bible those five words remain the same, "I will build My church!" The words were simple; the vision was clear. They were not hidden in verbosity. Jesus came to build His church.

Building requires:

- ▲ A plan (a vision): You must sit down and count the cost.
- ▲ A foundation (the apostles' doctrine): It is unshakable, built upon a solid rock not sand. Jesus is our chief cornerstone.
- ▲ Walls: Do not stop with the foundation. Continue in the apostles' doctrine.
- ▲ Financial investment: tithes and offerings. Count the cost and pay it.
- ▲ Work and determination: Give it your all—your best.
- ▲ Completion: Keep sowing until church growth happens and until the world is reached.

▲ Maintenance: Beginning in the Spirit, continue living godly in this evil world. Pray. Fast.

Isaiah 6 reveals three types of vision:

Upward vision	Isaiah 6:1-3
Inward vision	Isaiah 6:5
Outward vision	Isaiah 6:8

Wayne Cordeiro in *Doing Church as a Team* wrote, "Vision is the ability to see what others may not. It is the capacity to see potential—what things could be. Vision is the ability to see what God sees and the God-given motivation to bring what you see to pass!"

A favorite vision quote: "For those who dream, the road of life glistens with a million golden promises. To journey along that road, all that is needed is the strength to hold on to those dreams and the vision to see them through." (Caroline Gray)

Vision is faith. "Now faith is the substance of things hoped for, the evidence of things not seen" (Hebrews 11:1).

Each of us needs a vision in five areas:

Vision of Heaven	John 14:2-3
Vision of the value of a lost eternal soul	II Corinthians 4:3-4
Vision of Hell	Jude 23; Luke 16:19-31
Vision of a lost and dying world	Luke 19:10
Vision of the Lord of the harvest saying, "Well done!"	Matthew 25:21

After Adam and Eve transgressed in the Garden of Eden, God asked, "Adam, where art thou?" (Genesis 3:9). The same question could be asked of you, "Where are you?"

▲ What is your ministry?

- ▲ What is your vision?
- ▲ What is the will of God for your life?

Regardless of where we are, our age, or our gender, we each have three things in common. We have a past, present, and Lord willing, a future.

Past	Where have you been?
Present	Where are you now?
Future	Where are you going?

We need to make sure that we are more focused on where we are going than where we have been, more centered on our tomorrows than our yesterdays.

T. D. Jakes wrote that everyone has a date of entry (starting) in this world (birth date) and a date of departure (finishing) from this world (death date). All that is between the two is the – (dash). What are you putting in the dash between the time of your entry into this world and departure? On November 22, 1963, an assassin killed President John F. Kennedy. Kennedy's simple tombstone reads: 1917—1963.

Kennedy cast a vision for putting a rocket on the moon. On July 20, 1969, the United States launched a space rocket, landed it on the moon, and brought the crew home safely. This, like all compelling visions, requires four distinct qualities, according to James Davis:

- ▲ Purpose: Why should the vision be activated?
- ▲ Projection: When will the vision be achieved?
- ▲ Plan: How will the vision be accomplished?
- ▲ Promise: Who will benefit from the vision?

Jesus told Paul, "For I have appeared unto thee for this purpose" (Acts 26:16). He had an understanding of his purpose in life and ministry. Later Paul concluded, "I have fought a good fight, I have finished my course, I have kept the faith" (II Timothy 4:7).

How did Paul get this vision? He asked. "Who art thou, Lord" (Acts 9:5). "What wilt thou have me to do?" (Acts 9:6). The apostle Paul received his heavenly vision by asking, "Lord, what do you want me to do?" Throughout his lifetime, he continued to ask this same question. And we should too.

God spoke to Habakkuk, "Write the vision, and make it plain" (Habakkuk 2:2). Writing down the vision will help you remember what God said. Writing also brings about clarity. "Then the Lord said to me, 'Write my answer in large, clear letters on a tablet, so that a runner can read it and tell everyone else. But these things I plan won't happen right away. Slowly, steadily, surely, the time approaches when the vision will be fulfilled. If it seems slow, wait patiently, for it will surely take place. It will not be delayed'" (Habakkuk 2:2-3, NLT).

In Luke 1 a virgin named Mary was given a vision for her life. She would bring forth the Messiah and call His name Jesus. Naturally, Mary asked, "How shall this be?" The angel gave a brief explanation, "For with God nothing shall be impossible." It is important to know the *what* and leave the *how* up to God. Mary's attitude was pure. She said, "Be it unto me according to thy word." She was determined to step into a place of obedience regardless of the outcome.

Global Missions Director Bruce Howell often says, "Perhaps not in my lifetime." Vision is the ability to see beyond your lifetime. A God-given vision will outlive you. God gave David a dream. However, its destiny was committed into his son's hands. Both were in alignment with God's design. Through both generations, a house was built for God. Vision can be passed from one generation to the next. During the time of harvest, it is not uncommon to see three generations working the field. Like the words of prophecy that came forward at Because of the Times one year, "Meet you in the field!"

Sensibility

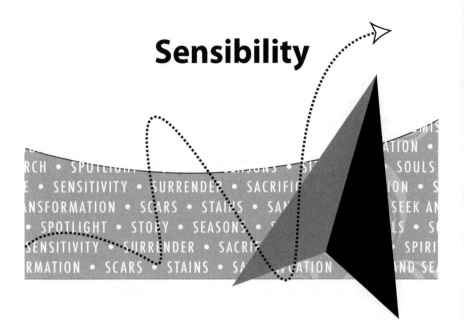

God has given us tremendous evaluative and investigative aids and tools. *Common sense* is "the capacity to reflect on different courses of action and to predict the likely implications of each." "But he must be . . . sober-minded (sensible, discreet), upright and fair-minded" (Titus 1:8, AMP).

Strange thing about tools: Sometimes they work, and sometimes they do not. You need the right tool for the occasion or task at hand. Warning: Sensing the will of God is not based entirely on *common sense* or evidence that is based on, "tradition, conventional wisdom, someone's philosophy or perspective." God told Philip to leave a mighty revival in Samaria to go to the desert. It did not make logical sense, but it was the right thing to do. Discovering the will of God requires more than "brain power." Still, there are certain aspects of life and God's will which should be easily discernable.

"Trust in the Lord with all your heart: do not depend on your own understanding. Seek his will in all you do, and he will direct your paths. Don't be impressed with your own wisdom" (Proverbs 3:5-7, NLT).

Dawson Trotman said, "God gave you an awful lot of leading when He gave you your mind." Do not expect divine guidance where/when common sense or simply reading God's Word would be enough.

Here's how you can use your brain:

- ▲ List options or alternatives.
- ▲ List benefits and advantages of each option (pros).
- ▲ List the consequences or disadvantages of each option (cons).
- ▲ List talents, abilities, and gifts you have to fulfill each option (Luke 14:31-32).
- ▲ List weaknesses, lack of skills, you have in meeting the demands of each option.
- ▲ List the circumstances involved.

Let's take an example from Acts 6.

They encountered a problem.	"Greek . . . widows were being discriminated against in the daily distribution of food" (Acts 6:1-2, NLT).
They considered the options.	"We . . . should spend our time preaching and teaching the word of God, not administering a food program" (Acts 6:2, NLT).
They explained the benefits.	"Then we can spend our time in prayer and preaching and teaching the word" (Acts 6:4, NLT).
They made a decision.	"Select seven men. . . . We will put them in charge of this business" (Acts 6:3, NLT).
They reaped the results.	"God's message was preached in ever-widening circles. The

	number of believers were greatly increased . . . and many of the Jewish priests were converted" (Acts 6:7, NLT).

Satisfaction

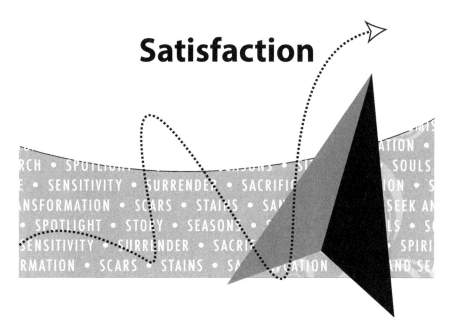

Doing God's will brings satisfaction and energy. "Jesus saith unto them, My meat is to do the will of him that sent me, and to finish the work" (John 4:34).

What fills your thoughts night and day? That is likely the will of God for you (if you are walking in the Spirit and putting away the lust of the flesh). Peace will come when you are in the perfect will of God. You want to cry out, "Yes! I was born to do this!"

David Livingstone said, "If you knew the satisfaction of performing a duty, as well as the gratitude to God which the missionary must always feel in being chosen for so noble and sacred a calling, you would feel no hesitation in embracing it. For my own part I have never ceased to rejoice that God has appointed me to such an office. People talk of the sacrifice I have made in spending so much of my life in Africa. Can that be called a sacrifice which is simply paid back as a small part of a great debt owing to our God, which we can never repay?"

Study

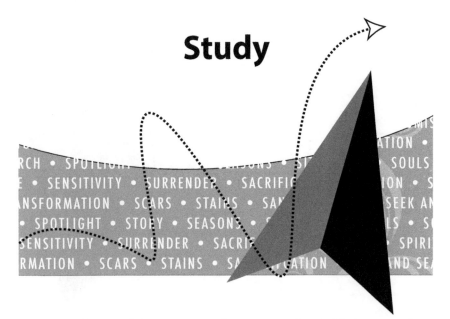

Someone has said, "Time spent sharpening the sickle is never time that is wasted."

"Study to shew thyself approved unto God, a workman that needeth not to be ashamed, rightly dividing the word of truth" (II Timothy 2:15).

Andy Stanley in his DVD series "Discovering God's Will" explained why it is so pivotal to study God's Word when seeking His will:

- ▲ We study His Word to find the big picture—God's plan for everything that happens.
- ▲ We study His Word to find the commands and law He gives for all to obey.
- ▲ The more we study and learn about God, the closer we get to Him.
- ▲ The closer we get to the understanding of who and what He is, the easier it is to make a decision about God's plan for our lives.

Howard Hendricks said, "The will of God is found in the Word of God. The more a person grows, the more he begins to think instructively and habitually from a divine perspective."

"Wherefore be ye not unwise, but understanding what the will of the Lord is" (Ephesians 5:17).

God will never provide guidance, or ask you to do anything that is contrary to His Word. "I will instruct thee and teach thee in the way which thou shalt go: I will guide thee with mine eye" (Psalm 32:8).

Do not go beyond what is written, "And these things, brethren, I have in a figure transferred to myself and to Apollos for your sakes; that ye might learn in us not to think of men above that which is written, that no one of you be puffed up for one against another" (I Corinthians 4:6).

Stay in the Word! Saturate yourself in the Word! As the hub keeps the wheel centered on the axle, so the Word of God keeps us centered on truth. The Bible is primarily and essentially the written will of God for our lives. Examine the Scriptures. The Bible is our guidebook in all things. God also provides certain unwritten directives, but obey God's written Word first (Psalms 1:2-3). Know God. Love God. He will make His will clear.

Remembering the Past; Promising the Future
by
Bruce A. Howell

As I co-chaired the Global Council, in Bangkok, Thailand, I was awed by the tremendous fellowship and heritage we possess within the United Pentecostal Church International. Directly in front of me sat Lee Sherry. Thirty-eight years ago, at the age of thirteen, he baptized me in the precious name of our Lord Jesus Christ. To my left sat Robert Rodenbush. At fifteen, I preached my first message in his church. My parents divorced when I was three, and my father died when I was ten. My mother, although familiar with the church as a young lady, fought against my being part of it. (Before her death,

81

however, she received the baptism of the Holy Ghost.) My wife, Diane, grew up in the church, and her grandfather was a minister. Together, we have a made-up mind, have never looked back, and are firmly committed and unwavering with the faith once delivered to the saints.

Given the opportunity, you have your own story to tell. Take a moment and reflect on it—the battles fought, the victories won, and your steadfast loyalty to apostolic doctrine and right living. By upholding truth and uncompromisingly preaching it, we will evangelize our world

I walked away from that meeting rejoicing in my heritage, thankful for what God is doing globally, and with a fresh commitment to world evangelism and to lifting high the banner of truth. I trust you will do the same!

God guides us as we search the Scriptures. "All scripture is given by inspiration of God, and is profitable for doctrine, for reproof, for correction, for instruction in righteousness: That the man of God may be perfect, thoroughly furnished unto all good works" (II Timothy 3:16-17).

John Wesley said, "It's [the Scripture is] how God teaches, rebukes, corrects, and trains us for the journey so we may be thoroughly equipped for every good work."

"But strong meat belongeth to them that are of full age, even those who by reason of use have their senses exercised to discern both good and evil" (Hebrews 5:14).

Stewardship

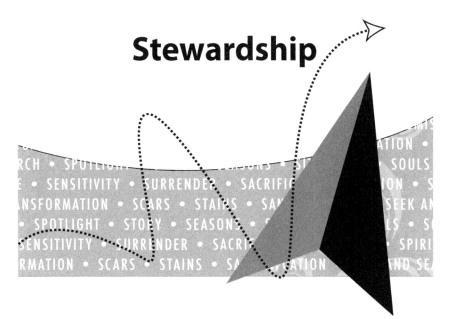

"Moreover it is required in stewards, that a man be found faithful" (I Corinthians 4:2).

Hold on! It is easy to skip through that verse and move on. Let's not miss the point. God expects—no requires—us to be faithful. He requires faithfulness in the small things. Interestingly, those that God selects to do great things for Him were usually found being faithful at small tasks. David was a shepherd boy. Nehemiah was a cupbearer. When you are faithful with the small things, trust is built; and God gives you bigger things to do. If you do your work well, God will give you something else to do. If you do not do your job well, do not be surprised when He takes the task from you and gives it to someone else to do. Do what you already know to be God's will.

Colleen Carter, in her lesson entitled "An Extra Set of Hands" lists the top twenty things she feels every faithful steward should have or be:

- ▲ Open mind
- ▲ Obedient
- ▲ Flexibility

- ▲ Honest
- ▲ Trustworthiness
- ▲ Determination
- ▲ Adaptability
- ▲ Sharp/attentive eyes
- ▲ Patience
- ▲ Redeemer of time
- ▲ Industrious
- ▲ Teachable spirit
- ▲ Diligence
- ▲ Passion
- ▲ Submission
- ▲ Cooperation and support
- ▲ Constant and consistent
- ▲ Servant's heart
- ▲ Respectfulness
- ▲ Willingness

"Whatsoever thy hand findeth to do, do it with thy might: for there is no work, nor device, nor knowledge, nor wisdom, in the grave, whither thou goest" (Ecclesiastes 9:10).

Kent Crockett in *Making Today Count for Eternity* provided the following explanation concerning faithfulness:

- ▲ Faithfulness means excellence—doing one's best in every situation.
- ▲ Faithfulness means integrity—being above moral reproach.
- ▲ Faithfulness means dependability—fulfilling commitments.
- ▲ Faithfulness means perseverance—enduring to the finish line.

God expects us to be faithful in every area of life. Here are some specifics:

Time	What is the priority for our time, and who gives us every	"The days of our years are threescore years and

	second? Each of us has a short life span. When our time is over, we will be judged by what we did for God.	ten; and if by reason of strength they be fourscore years, yet is their strength, labour and sorrow; for it is soon cut off, and we fly away. . . . So teach us to number our days, that we may apply our hearts to wisdom" (Psalm 90:10, 12).
Talent	How do we use the gifts God has given us (Matthew 25:14-30; Luke 19:12-27)? Jesus uses a parable to remind us that our place and service in Heaven will depend on the faithfulness of our lives and service on earth.	"And he said unto them, Take heed what ye hear: with what measure ye mete, it shall be measured to you: and unto you that hear shall more be given. For he that hath, to him shall be given: and he that hath not, from him shall be taken even that which he hath" (Mark 4:24-25).
Treasure	Where does God fit into our plan of giving? The first of our increase given to God proves we know and appreciate where everything comes from.	"Sell that ye have, and give alms; provide yourselves bags which wax not old, a treasure in the heavens that faileth not, where no thief approacheth, neither moth corrupteth. For where your treasure is, there will your heart be also" (Luke 12:33-34).

Testimony	How can we show others God's greatness? The way we live is a testimony of God's power and grace to keep us from sin.	"That in every thing ye are enriched by him, in all utterance, and in all knowledge; Even as the testimony of Christ was confirmed in you" (I Corinthians 1:5-6).
Tongue	How can we claim to love God if we do not talk of Him (James 3)? What we say can bless or curse, and needs to be given to God first.	"Keep thy tongue from evil, and thy lips from speaking guile" (Psalm 34:13). "I said, I will take heed to my ways, that I sin not with my tongue: I will keep my mouth with a bridle, while the wicked is before me" (Psalm 39:1).
Temple	Who needs our bodies presented as a living sacrifice? God lives in our hearts, and He wants our bodies to reflect His dwelling place in our lives.	"I beseech you therefore, brethren, by the mercies of God, that ye present your bodies a living sacrifice, holy, acceptable unto God, which is your reasonable service" (Romans 12:1). "What? Know ye not that your body is the temple of the Holy Ghost which is in you, which ye have of God, and ye are not your own? For ye are bought with a price:

		therefore glorify God in your body, and in your spirit, which are God's" (I Corinthians 6:19-20).

David J. Hesselgrove in *Planting Churches Cross-Culturally* quoted Ralph Martin, the author of *Worship in the Early Church*:

▲ The basis of stewardship is God has given abundantly to His children.
▲ The most important offering is committing one's life to God.
▲ All Christian giving should be voluntary and cheerful.
▲ Stewardship is offered in accordance to one's ability and the needs of others.
▲ God is no man's debtor.
▲ Churches and people should be open in providing accountability in all areas of stewardship.
▲ Concern for the welfare of others creates a bond of love between the giver and the recipient.

Ask yourself these questions taken from the *Daily Walk Study Bible:*

▲ Are you faithful in little things? Little responsibilities? Little promises? Small amounts of time, or talents (Luke 16:10)?
▲ Are you faithful with money (Luke 16:11)?
▲ Are you faithful with the associations of others (Luke 16:12)? Are you as careful of the properties and reputation of others as you are with your own?

What Are You Sending Ahead?
by
Bruce A. Howell

John Wesley once visited the estate of one of the wealthiest land owners of his time. They rode around the property for hours.

The land owner finally asked, "What do you think?" Wesley replied, "You are going to have a hard time leaving all of this."

We are pilgrims passing through this world. We cannot take anything with us when we go. We can however send eternal investments on ahead. Randy Alcorn calls it the "Treasure Principle." He uses the analogy of foreign businessmen that come to countries and stay for three months to work on a project. Living in a hotel room they are told they cannot carry anything back with them on the plane when their work is completed. They can send anything they earn by depositing it in the bank account in advance of their return. So what will they do? Purchase luxurious furniture and electronic equipment for the hotel room? I don't think so. They make an investment in their future.

The Bible speaks of sending our hearts and treasures ahead of us (Matthew 6:19-21; 1 Timothy 6:7). Mark it down: there is no way to separate the heart and its treasures. We send our treasures in advance. Our hearts soon follow. What is your treasure? Where is your heart? You will find them both in the same location. No wonder Alcorn says, "Anything we try to hang on to here will be lost: but anything we put in God's hands will become eternal treasure."

There is no greater investment than reaching lost souls. The investment quickly multiplies as they share the apostolic truth with their family and friends. Our frontline missionaries give all; risk all to make eternal investments in the many fields of the world. Our pastors and churches recognize their heart and unite with them to plow, plant, and produce the crop in each location. The harvest is our investment. It is our treasure. Kingdom investments reap kingdom dividends. Uncountable souls reached on earth equals stored treasure in heaven forever.

We give and go because there is a big harvest; a gigantic need. The field is the world. Investment opportunities abound. There can be no quitting now. General Patton once said, "I don't want to receive any message saying we are holding our position. We are advancing constantly. We're not interested in holding anything except the enemy."

Join our missionaries as they relentlessly labor to fulfill what was written about one man that went to some islands of the South Pacific. When the missionary died, this was placed on his grave:

> *When he came here,*
> *There were no Christians.*
> *When he went away,*
> *There were no heathen.*

The question doesn't come down to, what are you leaving behind? It is, what are you sending ahead?

Accomplishing a vision requires faithful stewardship of time, talents, and treasures. These are the prices on the road to success. Like the DaVinci Awards ad says, "Honoring those who have a will and have found a way." There is a divine will to be accomplished in the right way, and that requires faithful stewardship.

Dear Robert and Evangeline Rodenbush:

Today we were at the Community Eight assembly. Through the years you have been instrumental in opening nations to the truth. Only eternity will reveal how many souls have been reached, challenged, and changed through your ministry. Let me take a moment and highlight a couple.

Your little family stepped on Ghana's soil over forty years ago. One of the saints that stood by your side was J. Monnie. Did you ever know that generations later her twin granddaughters would be standing in a Pentecostal altar? Both their grandmother and mother have stepped into eternity. The girls stood dressed the same, hair fixed nearly the same, and received the baptism of the Holy Spirit simultaneously. Did you ever know that your obedience to a call would have a domino effect on succeeding generations?

Did you know that over twenty-five years ago, in the midst of office details as the coordinator of overseas ministries, as you took time to write a sensitive note, or make a kind comment, you would challenge my life toward continued commitment to missions?

When we get over there, one by one, from West African nations, from Europe to the Middle East, and the many nations where you've ministered, precious souls will greet you with a question, "Did you ever know?"

Taking the Word to the world,

Jim Poitras

Service/Servanthood

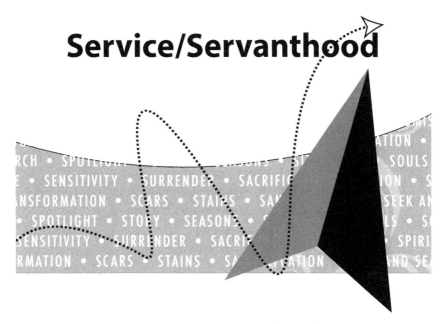

Service/Servanthood

"But he that is greatest among you shall be your servant" (Matthew 23:11). The Greek word used for *servant* means "to run an errand, to be an attendant, to wait upon a host, teacher, friend."

Arthur Ashe said, "True heroism is remarkably sober, very undramatic. It is not the urge to surpass all others at whatever cost, but the urge to serve at whatever the cost."

The poem that follows was written during a time in my life that I was desperately endeavoring to discern God's will concerning my vocation and location. It identifies the bottom line; God is in control.

My Constant Prayer

Lord,
I am Your servant.
Place me wherever I can be of most service to You,
With the talents and ministry You have given to me.

I am Your living sacrifice.
You alone are the Boss.
You are in control of my life;
Let me see clearly the vision,
Hear and sense Your will,
And walk uprightly in the footsteps You have for me.

I want to know You
And be in constant touch with You.
Help me keep my priorities correct:
Love You,
Love my family,
Love my world.

I'm reaching for You.
Reaching for Your constant will.
Reaching my family,
Sojourners on the road of life,
Reaching the lost . . .
Reaching!

"I don't know what your destiny will be, but one thing I know: the only ones among you who will be truly happy are those who will have sought and found how to serve." (Albert Schweitzer)

The baptism of the Holy Spirit is an integral part of the salvation plan provided to mankind. It does not stop at our salvation, but empowers us to be of service in God's kingdom.

Dimension	Purpose	Bless	Kingdom	Who?	Results	Scripture
Salvation	To save	I am blessed.	Adding to the Kingdom.	This is for me.	I am part of the harvest.	Acts 2:38; 47
Service	To send	I am a blessing.	Advancing the Kingdom.	This is for them.	I help.	Acts 1:8

"But you shall receive power (ability, efficiency, and might) when the Holy Spirit has come upon you, and you shall be My witnesses in Jerusalem and all Judea and Samaria and to the ends (the very bounds) of the earth" (Acts 1:8, AMP).

Jim George in *God's Man of Influence* offered nine insights on establishing a servant ministry. They included:

- ▲ Serve for a higher purpose (I Thessalonians 2:1).
- ▲ Serve in spite of your situation (I Thessalonians 2:2).
- ▲ Serve with integrity (I Thessalonians 2:3).
- ▲ Serve to please God (I Thessalonians 2:4).
- ▲ Serve with pure motives (I Thessalonians 2: 5-6).
- ▲ Serve with love (I Thessalonians 2:7-8).
- ▲ Serve sacrificially (I Thessalonians 2:9).
- ▲ Serve blamelessly (I Thessalonians 2:10).
- ▲ Serve to nurture (I Thessalonians 2:11-12).

Understanding that we are servants is simple. To actually serve; that is a problem. It does not fit into the world's view of leadership nor does it please the desires of the flesh. We must constantly strive to be the servant that God wants us to be.

We need to remember that serving others is part of our God-given responsibility. Shirley Chisholm, the first African-American woman to win a seat in the United States Congress said, "Service is the rent we pay for living." In the playing field of Christianity we need to be participators rather than spectators. Too many times we possess a "serve-us" mentality instead of a service mindset.

We are called to serve!

Strengths

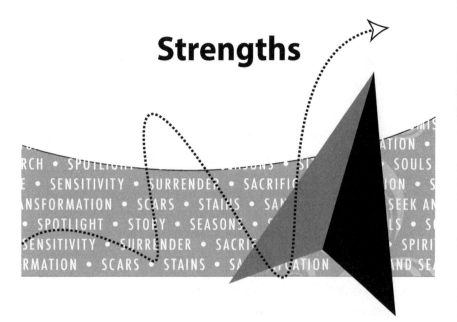

Each one is given talents, gifts of the Spirit, to be of service in God's kingdom. Each one has strengths and weaknesses. The tendency is to spend time developing weaknesses. That only enables you to be mediocre. Spend time developing your talents, and you will excel. God will provide a place for you to use your unique gifting in His kingdom.

"And who knoweth whether thou art come to the kingdom for such a time as this?" (Esther 4:14).

Lisa Jefferson, the phone supervisor who took Todd Beamer's call from United Flight 93 before it crashed in rural Pennsylvania on 9/11, said, "I believe that God used me as a messenger for the Beamer family and to deliver God's message the way He wanted it to be delivered, and I'm pretty sure God used me for that reason. You know, God has an assignment for you that only you can fulfill. And I think God uses us as we are with our unique gifts, abilities, and experiences. And I wasn't prepared for my test on September 11th. I went on faith and made myself available. God is not concerned about your ability, but your availability."

Know your ministry. The Lord usually uses us in our area of

giftedness (Romans 12:6-8; I Corinthians 12:1-11; Ephesians 4:11-13). What you enjoy best could be indicative of God's will for your life.

Suffering

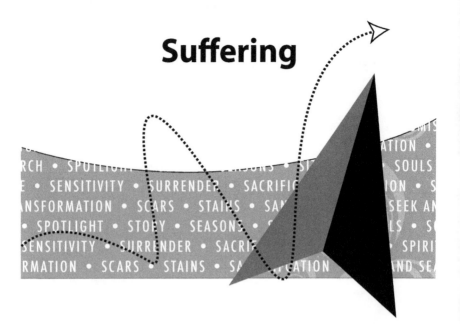

Bad things happening to us does not mean that we are out of the will of God (Romans 8:28). Ask Job. Suffering does not mean that we are out of the will of God (I Peter 3:17; 4:19). Ask Paul. Bad things make us what and who we are. When we suffer, we become more sensitive to the needs of others and what they are going through. Jesus understands what we are passing through. He was tempted and overcame (Hebrews 4:15; Luke 4). Sometimes the little nuisances and difficulties cause us to want to give up. They become like sand in our shoes. Bad situations change. No condition is permanent. This too shall pass!

"[For my determined purpose is] that I may know Him [that I may progressively become more deeply and intimately acquainted with Him, perceiving and recognizing and understanding the wonders of His Person more strongly and more clearly], and that I may in that same way come to know the power outflowing from His resurrection [which it exerts over believers], and that I may so share His sufferings as to be continually transformed [in spirit into His likeness even] to His death, [in the hope]" (Philippians 3:10, AMP).

God's call, will, and vision may require suffering. "Wherefore let them that suffer according to the will of God commit the keeping of their souls to him in well doing, as unto a faithful Creator" (I Peter 4:19).

Warren and David Wiersbe in *Ten Power Principles for Christian Service* advised the following about suffering:

- ▲ Expect it (1 Peter 4:12; John 15:18, 20).
- ▲ Accept it as God's gift (Philippians 1:29).
- ▲ Evaluate it and yield to God's purposes (Job 23:10).
- ▲ Learn to live a day at a time and give your cares to God (Psalms 69:19; I Peter 5:7).
- ▲ Trust God to turn suffering into eternal glory (II Corinthians 4:17).

From Here to There
by
Bruce A. Howell

Forewarning: These words may not be for you . . . yet. I address a select group of people—those, around the world, who feel they are taking three steps forward and two steps back. At heart, missionaries are conquerors, ever ready to respond to the challenge of reaching nations for Christ. But at times the conqueror feels conquered. I'm not whining or complaining, just facing reality. We work in environments we did not create and find difficult to change. What do we do in such cases?

1. Jesus said, "Upon this rock I will build my church; and the gates of hell shall not prevail against it" (Matthew 16:18). That's the bottom line. It's His church and not ours, an apt reminder in good times and consoling in not-so-good times.

2. Three steps forward and two steps back is progress. Change seldom happens at the lightning speed we prefer. The organizational structure we work with may have a unique characteristic. One man cannot swiftly topple it. One man cannot hastily revolutionize it. In time, "church evolution" takes place. Things gradually improve as we strive for perfection. It is essential to assemble a team of change agents, cast the vision, and work toward it despite the walls of resistance. Sound the alarm when you see the church isn't moving forward. However, even setbacks may be development in disguise or may lead to progress.

3. The strength of a man consists in finding out the way God is going and going that direction. How do we move from where we are to where we want to go? Keep our eyes fixed on the destination. Have a travel plan.

4. It is difficult to see progress during a single day, but it becomes obvious when looking back over the long haul. Keep a diary or list of victories. "Count your blessings. Name them one by one. It will surprise you what the Lord has done." (Edwin Othello Excell Johnson, Jolene Boyd Oatman)

5. Encourage fellow sojourners who may be struggling. Our place on this earth is not to see through others, but to see others through.

Dan Southerland in Transitioning explained four factors for consideration in moving (churches) from here to there.

- **The distance you must go.** The farther you are going, the slower you must move. Turnarounds require time.
- **The size of the ship.** The bigger the church or change, the slower you must go. It takes thirteen miles to turn an oil tanker around.
- **The age of the ship.** The older the church, the slower change should be implemented.
- **The toughness of the leaders.** The tougher the leaders are who are implementing the change the faster you can go. Leaders should be tough enough to lead, but gentle enough to care.

Never lose your vision. Don't give up. You can make it. Remember,

Suffering or trouble can be for our benefit because they strengthen us as Christians. "It takes a world with trouble in it to train men and women for their high calling as children of God. Faced with trouble, some people (like Joseph) grow wings; others buy crutches. Which kind are you?" *(Daily Walk Bible)*.

Specific

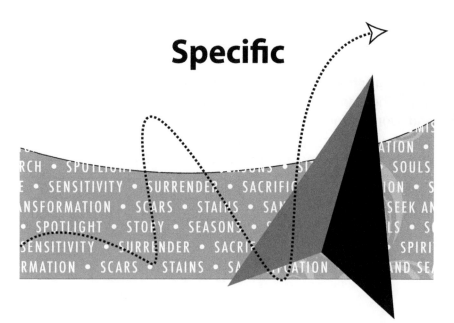

God's will can be general or specific. His general will is clearly revealed throughout Scripture. But many people have difficulty sensing His specific will. The general will of God encompasses the things He desires for us. Basically, it is referring to obeying His commandments. They apply to everybody. Repent, be baptized in Jesus' name, and receive the Holy Spirit. Do not lie, cheat, or steal. Pray without ceasing. Have exemplary ethics, morals, and lifestyle. Got the point?

God's specific will applies to specific people in specific ways. Every decision should be compatible with God's Word. Any decisions that contradict His Word should be discarded. God never leads us to violate His commands.

"So then do not be foolish but understand what the will of the Lord is" (Ephesians 5:17).

It is important to read the Bible daily. It becomes our anchor, guidepost, and the lens which better enables us to sense the specific will of God. Search the Scriptures, and you will find God's general will. He primarily speaks to us through His Word. It is an "open book" test. "Lo, I come (in the volume of the book it is written of me,) to do thy will, O God" (Hebrews 10:7). Remember, that *testament* means "will." God's will is God's Word. It unveils His purposes, intentions, and desires.

So start with the will you already know, do that, and move on to the specific will of God. One of the best indicators as to whether a person is willing to follow God's will, is whether or not he is following what he already knows, as it is revealed in the Bible.

Many focus on the specific will more than the general will. That is backwards—the proverbial cart before the horse.

Some advocate the "open door" policy of finding God's will. Walk through the doors that open to you, and do not break down the ones that are closed. This can also become the "open mine shaft" philosophy. Satan also opens doors. Many of these lead to destruction. Additionally, as your ministerial gifts make room for you, and you become more identified in the body of Christ, many doors—good doors—will open to you. Which ones should you take advantage of?

Ryan Shaw in *Momentum* said, "Too many wait around for some extraordinary demonstration to confirm God's will for their lives. Instead we should begin moving in the direction Scripture confirms is His general will; and as we do, He will confirm the specifics for us." He went on to say, "The Great Commandment and the Great Commission illustrate the supreme purposes of God. In seeking the will of God, we will not go wrong in committing ourselves to these two purposes."

Pierced Hearts
by
Bruce A. Howell

Global Nomads bear the marks of their cross-cultural experiences—mostly positive and occasionally negative— throughout life. The marks are seldom visible, but they are there just the same. Anyone involved in the sights and sounds of another culture and reaching the lost is never quite the same again. It is as if an arrow has pierced our hearts. We've been marked—heart, mind, and soul. I have been thinking about pierced hearts as I am writing this close to Valentine's Day. At this time of year, I often picture an arrow shooting a gigantic heart. I also think of my list of loved ones which includes my precious wife, Diane, my kids, grandkids, and my Global Nomad friends. Oh yeah, there is one more group on my list— our lost world.

Remember it was love (I John 4:7-8) that brought salvation to us (John 3:16; 15:13), and love that took us to the mission field. Only through love (and God's grace) do we manage to cope and remain on the field. Jesus said the first commandment was to love the Lord. The second is to love others (Mark 12:29-31). By this mark all will know that we are true disciples (John 13:34-35). Love is not merely a word; it is action (I John 3:16-19). The world doesn't fully understand true love, only lust which is self-seeking, self-centered, and self-satisfying. Lust asks, "What can I get?" Love asks, "What can I give?" Oops! Sounds like I'm preachin' so I better get back on track here.

Steve Green sings:
To love the Lord our God
Is the heartbeat of our mission,
("The Mission," by John Mohn and Randall Dennis)

Interestingly, Steve not only captivates our mission, but reflects someone who has been marked for life. He is a Global Nomad, raised by missionary parents in South America until he was eighteen. He recently commented, "I have spent my life trying to safeguard myself, building walls of security, independence, and provision, but God has spent my life undoing me. The reason He dismantles these walls is because I'm prone to trust what I know, and God is committed to keeping me weak, looking to Him." Marks in life keep us fragile and our eyes fixed on Jesus.

What marks did Steve Green's missionary encounters leave on his heart? Years ago he sang and made popular, "People Need the Lord." Yes, I recognize I am dating myself as that song may be before your time, but it still has a powerful message. It puts it all into perspective—from a pierced heart to pierced hearts. The song continues, "Through His love our hearts can feel all the grief they bear!"

Another group of Christian artists you may be familiar with is Selah—three gifted musicians that include a brother and sister brought up in the heartland of Africa. They can't get away from their roots and do an African song or two on each project. A recent article released by Curb Records explained that Jim Smith, following in his father's footsteps, took his family to a life of missionary work in the Congo. Todd, Nicol, and two other children grew "to see the world as a place of trees—mango, palm, and coconut—many planted by their grandmother. . . . They came to know the Congolese people, to speak their Kituba language, and to love their music." Nicol expressed her heart, "When you need to be comforted, there is nothing like these hymns, because so many of them were written from a place of suffering."

Perhaps, you can relate to this experience: "Our dad drove a seven-ton army truck, the only kind that would make it on those muddy roads in the rainy season. We'd have to cross these bridges made of six planks, forty feet above the river, and we'd always pray that the planks wouldn't break under the truck. That's what life was like there. You had to pray—just to survive."

I may not agree with their doctrinal slant—or even be aware of it—and I'm not promoting their music or starting the Howell Record Company. I am not even sure I always like their style. What attracts me to them is that they are missionary kids—Global Nomads. They are marked for life, and it shows through in their lyrics and musical expression in their interviews and articles. They have found a way to express their pierced hearts and to bless others. I pray that each Global Nomad throughout the United Pentecostal Church

International will do the same. Many of you are equally talented and can, and will, impact our church and our world.

> *Here's my advice:*
> *Love the Lord your God.*
> *Love others. It is the heartbeat of our mission.*
> *You are marked for life. Thank God for it!*
> *Your heart has been pierced. It is for a purpose.*
> *You cannot lead others where you have never been.*
> *Your pain is the seed of healing for the hurting.*
> *Find outlets for your experiences and bless your world.*
> *People need the Lord!*

"How can we understand the road we travel? It is the Lord who directs our steps" (Proverbs 20:24, NLT).

Selected

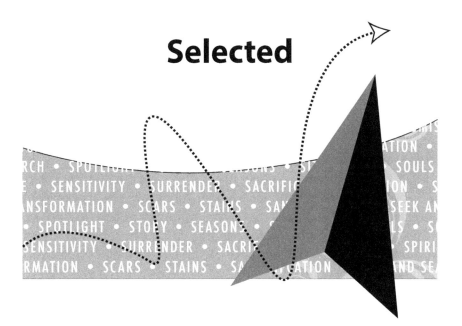

In the midst of all the mind-boggling stuff and images in the Book of Revelation I find several things easy to comprehend. I see a clearer picture of Heaven, our final destination. There, our missions endeavors culminate as "all nations will come and worship before..." the Lamb (Revelation 15:4).

I like it when I read, "the Lamb shall overcome them: for he is Lord of lords, and King of kings: and they that are with him are called, and chosen, and faithful" (Revelation 17:14).

Those that are with Him are identified as called, chosen, and faithful. This is the first—and only—time that these three words appear together. The called, chosen, and faithful have sold all, and given all, to buy into the harvest field. They are treasures and treasured. They are preparing today, for that day, when the gathered ones will sing, "You are worthy to take the scroll and to open its seals, because you were slain, and with your blood you purchased men for God from every tribe and language and people and nation" (Revelation 5:9, NIV).

Because of the called, chosen, and faithful there will be "a great multitude that no one can count, from every nation, tribe, people and language, standing before the throne and in front of the Lamb" (Revelation 7:9, NIV). That is one of the only mental pictures that trumps the feeling I get when missionaries march into the conference auditorium with unfurled flags from around the world.

You are called: not only out of darkness into His marvelous light (1 Peter 2:9), but called to take the truth to the ends of the earth. Dr. Thomas Addinton and Dr. Stephen Graves wrote an excellent little book entitled *A Case for Calling*. In it they define "calling" as: "God's personal invitation for me to work on his agenda, using the talents I've been given in ways that are eternally significant." Calling is what we do to fit into God's purpose. It is a privilege to be part of His divine agenda.

You are "called according to his purpose" (Romans 8:28). God "hath saved us, and called us with an holy calling, not according to our works, but according to his own purpose..." (2 Timothy 1:9). "I therefore, beseech you that ye walk worthy of the vocation wherewith ye are called" (Ephesians 4:1).

We are part of the church, the called out ones. The Greek word utilized was originally used among the Greeks to identify a body of citizens that have gathered to discuss affairs. Together, we proceed full speed ahead with the King's business; reaching the world.

You are chosen: I suppose there are many that receive a call into missions, but do not respond. I've known a few such people myself. A vast array of reasons can keep someone from answering the call. To be chosen, one must respond to the call. The Global Missions Board confirms the call resident and evident in the life of a missionary candidate.

What an honor to be chosen by God to be His disciples and to work with Him in the harvest. The chosen are "in Christ Jesus" (Romans 8:1) and have "put on the Lord Jesus" (Romans 13:14,

NKJV). We choose to put God first in our lives, put God's Word into daily practice, and refuse to become entangled in the affairs of this life. We have another world in view.

You are faithful: You are overcomers, more than conquerors, and triumphant. You stand faithfully in the Lord despite trials, tribulations, sufferings, adversities, afflictions, persecutions, and conflicts. You are trustworthy and continue in the faith. You are grounded and settled, refusing to move away from the hope of the gospel (Colossians 1:23).

You are the doers of God's Word and are making your calling and election sure (2 Peter 1:10). You made –and make—a choice. It is not a one time thing. We commit to the choice daily and persevere to the end. As we remain loyal to God we truly become the called, chosen, and faithful.

David Fraser said, "To rule with Christ in his kingdom, we must *hear* God's calling, *respond* to the calling with a changed life and be *faithful* to that calling until the end of life."

Steadfast

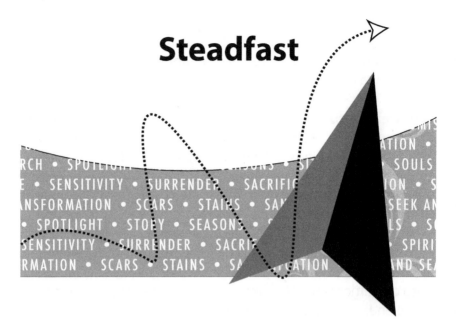

"And they continued steadfastly in the apostles' doctrine and fellowship, and in breaking of bread, and in prayers" (Acts 2:42).

Henry T. and Richard Blackaby in their *Experiencing God Day-by-Day* devotional quoted, "Now it came to pass, when the time had come for Him to be received up, that He steadfastly set His face to go to Jerusalem" (Luke 9:51).

They continued, "It is easy to become distracted in the Christian life! The moment you understand what God wants you to do, it will seem as though everyone around you requires your time and attention! When the time came for Jesus to go to the cross, He 'set His face' toward Jerusalem, so that nothing would prevent Him from accomplishing His Father's will. So obvious was His resolve to go to Jerusalem that the Samaritans, who hated the Jews, rejected Him because they recognized that He was a Jew traveling through their village to the hated city of Jerusalem.

"Jesus determined not to digress from His mission, but He took time to minister to many people along His way. He sent out seventy disciples into the surrounding towns (Luke 10:1). He healed lepers (Luke 17:11-19). He cured a man of dropsy (Luke

14:1-4). He continued to teach His disciples (Luke 15:1-32). Jesus did not refuse to minister to others as He went to Calvary, but ultimately He refused to be deterred from His Father's will.

"If you know what God wants you to do, set your sights resolutely toward that goal with full determination to accomplish it (Proverbs 4:25). Your resolve to go where God is leading ought to be evident to those around you. Beware of being so sidetracked by the opportunities around you that you lose sight of God's ultimate goal for you. Do not succumb to the temptation to delay your obedience or to discard it altogether. Once you have received a clear assignment from God, your response should be unwavering obedience."

They Continued...
by
Bruce A. Howell

After the dynamic, initial blastoff of the New Testament church in Acts 2, four words bring us from then and there to here and now. They are simple but directional: "And they continued steadfastly" (Acts 2:42). Need it simpler than that? "They continued!" The advancing church did not stop in Acts 2. It started there. It continues from there.

A Microsoft Word synonym check on steadfastly *brought up these words: "persistently, consistently, with conviction, unwaveringly, unfalteringly, loyally, and faithfully." Dr. Luke's placement of the two twin words "continued steadfastly" in rapid fire is strategic. Continued means "sustained, constant, continual, continuous, nonstop, unrelenting, unremitting, and persistent."*

The missionaries and Christians of Acts were men and women of perseverance. They refused to quit. They would not retreat. Forward ever; backward never. They held high the banner of truth with unwavering, unfaltering, unrelenting, unremitting conviction.

It wasn't that they did not have reason to turn back. One overarching reason caused them to press forward in the face of persecution, sacrifice, and alienation from their family and society. They unyieldingly believed that the promise (Acts 1:8) extended "to all that are afar off" (Acts 2:39). They had one goal in mind. They were forever pressing to the ends of the earth.

May the "whole gospel to the whole world" never become a well-worn cliché, but may it remain our undying passion. I unflinchingly assert that it is your only reason for continuation in your field of service. It is the only thing that will keep you focused as you navigate the interstates and back roads after prolonged months on the deputation trail. Lose the focus—whether at home or abroad—and you will begin to waver, flounder, falter, and be tempted to pull out the white handkerchief of defeat and surrender.

What do you do when the guts to continue diminishes in the daily drudgery of difficulties? What do you do when passion is depleted? Paul said it best: "Stir it up!" (II Timothy 1:6). Fan it into a flame! The spark of excitement and enthusiasm will be reignited. Peter added, "But the God of all grace, who hath called us unto his eternal glory by Christ Jesus, after that ye have suffered a while, make you perfect, stablish, strengthen, settle you" (I Peter 5:10).

Prayer changes things. Prayer changes you! God will establish you through restoring your vision and giving you renewed direction. You will not waver. You will be steadfast! He will strengthen you, place you on a firm foundation, and securely ground you. He will settle you, support you, and confirm your calling. You'll be perfect; nothing defective will be in you. He will set right what has gone wrong. He will put things in order for you. He'll give you the needed courage regardless of what happens.

Harvesters, remember: "So let's not allow ourselves to get fatigued doing good. At the right time we will harvest a good crop if we don't give up, or quit" (Galatians 6:9, MSG).

Avoid doctrinal perversion, like the plague it really is. Allow God's Word to serve as your anchor. Do not be moved away from the truth. "Therefore we ought to give the more earnest heed to the things which we have heard, lest at any time we should let them slip" (Hebrews 2:1).

Do not let the storms coming your way deter you from doing the Lord's will. "He that observeth the wind shall not sow; and he that regardeth the clouds shall not reap. As thou knowest not what is the way of the spirit, nor how the bones do grow in the womb of her that is with child: even so thou knowest not the works of God who maketh all. In the morning sow thy seed, and in the evening withhold not thine hand: for thou knowest not whether shall prosper, either this or that, or whether they both shall be alike good" (Ecclesiastes 11:4-6).

Devoted for Life
by
Bruce A. Howell

While in Burma, pioneer missionary Adoniram Judson suffered the death of his wife and child; the death of his second wife; he was imprisoned and in poor health. Yet he wrote, "The motto of every missionary . . . ought to be 'devoted for life.'" He endured so much, but kept running the mission's race.

Else Lund's retirement letter recalled one night at Fassama, Liberia. "A group of us were returning from a village service at Bella Balma about an hour and a half walk one way. We were walking single file as the path was very narrow; and some were talking as loudly as possible, probably to scare away any wild animals. Some were carrying lanterns, and some of us flashlights. Then I thought to myself, I could spend the rest of my life here. It was so satisfying carrying the gospel to the uttermost parts of the earth." Thanks, Missionary Lund for over forty-two years of running the mission's race.

I have a friend with a unique collection—old shoes. That's right. He has several treasured shoes received from seasoned missionaries. His array of tattered shoes is a reminder that we can run the race, finish strong, and hear, "Well done, thou good and faithful servant."

Bill Taylor, in Send Me! wrote an article, "Those Old Shoes Still Do It for Me!" He keeps a pair of old shoes on his desk. They remind him of an old runner now in his final lap of years well lived. When asking for the old shoes, Bill commented, "I want tangible shoe-leather evidence of how to finish well after all your years of life."

Taylor's faithful friend, his dad, served as a missionary in Latin America, then twelve years as CEO of his mission's agency in the States, and after that met their global missions board to ask for an appointment to Spain. The chairman of the stunned board retorted, "Sir, no president of a bank ever returns to become a teller." His dad quietly answered, "I do not work in a bank." They spent five years in Spain, and then returned to Atlanta to start seven Spanish-speaking churches.

My hat is off to the lifers in the United Pentecostal Church International. You are a rare breed and leave a tremendous heritage to us—shoes well-worn and difficult to fill. I want to run the race, finish the course, and receive this testimony, "Devoted for life!"

Stickability

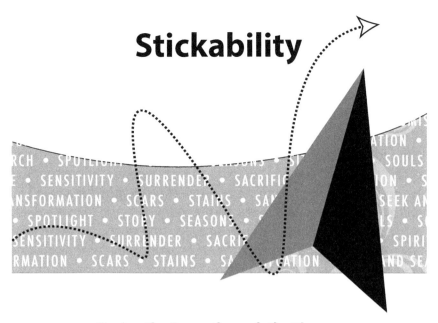

Seeing the Roses through the Thorns
by
Bruce A. Howell

My target is clearly in focus. You are there in our vast global harvest field, feeling the frustration, irritation, and pain of a spiritual thorn in your side or a splinter in your finger. I have prayed for you and desperately want to encourage you. Thorns and splinters are a barbed branch of our personal, spiritual, and ministerial growth process.

Like any field, thorns come with the territory. So what will we do with these prickly problems? It's basic. Identify the problem. Turn to the Word. Turn to prayer. Look to God. His grace is sufficient.

Another missionary experienced what we often feel. He contentedly stated, "There was given me a thorn (a splinter) in the flesh, a messenger of Satan, to rack and buffet and harass me" (II Corinthians 12:7, AMP). Paul went on to say, "Since I know it is all for Christ's good, I am quite content with my weaknesses and with insults, hardships, persecutions, and calamities. For when I am weak, then I am strong" (II Corinthians 12:10, NLT).

Paul's thorn—a messenger of Satan—was designed to discourage, derail, and destroy him. Its intent was to hinder his work, annihilate his influence, and stunt the growth of the church. Paul prayed God would remove this impediment.

Satan does his best to pull us down. But we are not ignorant of his tactics (II Corinthians 2:11). The ironic thing is this: he succeeds, yet fails because he pushes us to our knees. Prayer is the best remedy for any trouble. It gives us fresh perspective. It puts the proverbial ball in God's court. Paul accepted his thorn as a gift. Great success causes great retaliation. Opposition to the gospel is reason for encouragement and evidence that the Spirit of God is at work. The devil fights feverishly to preserve his falling and failing kingdom.

What are your thorns? The list could be lengthy. Unfortunately, some thorns are not just things, but people. I'll leave it to you to fill in the blank: My thorn in the flesh is _____.

Paul recognized problems for what they were and also saw his own shortcomings. He proceeded despite both disclosures. It takes God's grace to deal with sharp situations without becoming cynical, negative, fearful, vindictive, or revengeful. Paul's limitations cut him down to size and built him up to deeper dependence on his able God. When under the pinch of pain before yelling, "Ouch!" look for the positive. Accept problems as gifts that make you better instead of curses that make you bitter. Thorns strengthen, stretch, perfect, clarify motives, and check our commitment level. So please don't be tempted to pull out your white handkerchief and start waving it while shouting, "I surrender. I give up. Send me somewhere else!"

Faced with trouble, some grow wings; others buy crutches. Some see lemonade, others see a lemon. Some see roses, others only thorns.

May the Lord help us to see the roses through the thorns.

"But ye, brethren, be not weary in well doing" (II Thessalonians 3:13).

"If thou faint in the day of adversity, thy strength is small" (Proverbs 24:10).

Keep doing what you are doing:

- ▲ Read your Bible
- ▲ Study
- ▲ Pray
- ▲ Fast
- ▲ Obey

Stick with the vision. Do not allow it to be aborted.

Do not ever give up.

I Had a Dream!
by
Bruce A. Howell

A sprawled slogan on the back of a taxi in an overseas major metropolis caught my attention and stirred my mind. It boldly proclaimed, "I Had a Dream." Surely it was a mistake.

Everyone knows the famous words from Martin Luther King's renowned speech, "I have a dream." On second thought, maybe the taxi owner meant had. He had a dream, and the ragtag vehicle was the prize. Not much of a dream. I wonder how many of us, as we embark into another year, would be brave enough to admit, we had a dream. We left it behind in the lost and found department. What happened that faded, sidelined, or shipwrecked our God-given dream?

Check out conversations with ministerial friends. If most of the discussion is on past accomplishments rather than future projections, it is time to wake up your dream! H. Dale Burke in Less is More Leadership wrote, "When your memories are more exciting than your dreams, you've begun to die." Charles Hedges in Getting the Right Things Right said, "A dream is not something that you wake up from, but something that wakes you up."

Impossible things begin with extreme dreamers. Consider King's dream of a color-blind civilization. We have high aspirations— global impact, a reached world, pace-setting evangelism techniques that break through closed doors, churches abounding, and millions transformed.

Walt Kallestad in Wake Up Your Dreams said, "Great dreams require digging beyond surface limitations or past failures or easy-way-out distractions. . . . Dreams can help us see the invisible, believe the incredible, and achieve the impossible." He went on to say, "The only waste of time is to live a lifetime and never take the time to dream— to focus it, to plan for it, to live it."

Achieving dreams is tough business. It is much easier to live in mediocrity. But you never accomplish much in the stagnant, safe sector. Kallestad advised, "Every great dream involves tough climbing, but every great dream outlasts the tough climb." So get up, pick up your dream, and start climbing!

Mission possible: I challenge you to write down your ministry and personal dreams on three-by-five cards or display them on a laminated sheet. Read these often and work toward accomplishment daily.

Step

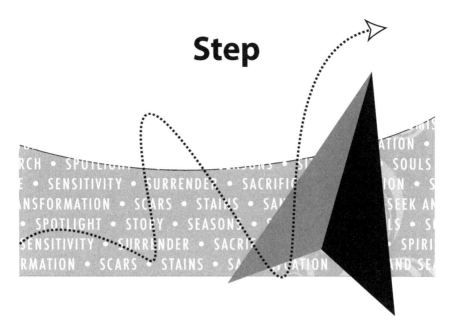

"The steps of a good man are ordered by the LORD: and he delighteth in his way" (Psalm 37:23).

The will of God is a continual step in the right direction. Being out of the will of God pulls you downward and further away from God. Jonah was called to the city of Nineveh. Instead of making steps toward it, he ran from it. Instead of running to God, he ran away from Him. This took Jonah down. In the belly of a big fish Jonah prayed for the will of God to be done. God is able to put us in situations where we will be delighted to do His will. The will of God is progressive and moves us closer to God. Being out of the will of God pulls us downward and further away from God.

Note Jonah's downward plunge:

- ▲ Down to Joppa (Jonah 1:3)
- ▲ Down into the ship (Jonah 1:5)
- ▲ Down into the sea (Jonah 1:15)
- ▲ Down into the belly of the big fish (Jonah 1:17)

David Livingstone said, "Without Christ, not one step; with Him, anywhere!"

I'm not sure why finding the will of God is so difficult. But, it is. It's as complex at eighteen as it is at fifty-two or seventy-three years of age. You would think that it would be only a colossal task for teenagers making their journey in life. I guess that unveils the secret right there. It is summed up in the word "journey." Too often we focus on the will of God as the destination, the completed journey, the pot of gold at the end of the rainbow. Our focus is faulty. The journey is never over as long as we have breath to breathe and a heart to do something for God and His people. We mistakenly focus on the road in the distance and bypass watching the single steps.

The journey—the Christian walk—has always been about traveling from one place to another. Like any journey it takes time; a long time. The road is etched with ups and downs. Occasional tough times meet our moving onward and upward. There are mountains and valleys. Sometimes we falter. Sometimes we fall. But, we get up and keep on going.

Like Kathryn Scott beautifully penned, "We still believe and though the journey has been hard we will confess your goodness…" I love it when she sings from "soaring wings to the shattered dream."

So, what is the will of God? It's not so much about the destination as it is about the journey. Amazingly, "By faith Abraham obeyed when he was called to go out to a place that he was to receive as an inheritance. And he went out, not knowing where he was going" (Hebrews 11:8, ESV). Was it some sort of blind faith or ruthless, risky abandonment? Probably not! He just took the next right step. The will of God is all about taking the next right step. We don't have to know twenty steps or ten miles down the road. Just get a grip on the next step. God told Abram, "Go." And he went. He journeyed one step at a time.

Like the heroes of Hebrews 11, we are all pilgrims on this planet. They believed. They had faith. They trusted in God's promises.

They obeyed His Word; the road map in life. So it is with us. We are not moving aimlessly or living without direction; walking around in circles. Our steps are ordered. They are established. Remember, "The steps of a good man are ordered by the Lord, And He delights in his way" (Psalms 37:23, NKJV). We are walking in step with God. He blazes the trail. It sounds so easy. It is. However, we make it difficult. How? By trying to see the whole trip instead of today's instructions.

Abraham's servant testified, "As for me, the Lord has led me on the journey" (Genesis 24:27, NIV). How did that happen? The answer is simple. He heard from the master. He embarked on a journey. He believed he would accomplish his purpose. He found the will of God one step at a time.

So, as you endeavor to seek and sense God's direction concentrate on taking the next right step!

Strategy

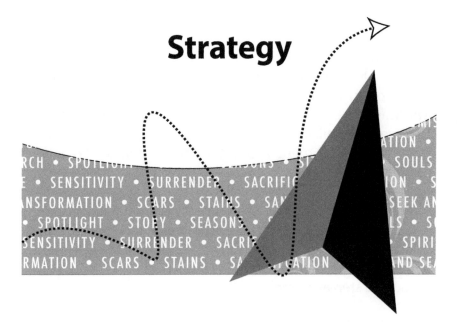

The idea of a strategy is borrowed from the military. It refers to moving troops into position before engaging the enemy. Strategy is:

▲ a plan of action to get a person from here to there.
▲ concerned with how you will achieve or accomplish the vision.
▲ important in realizing God's direction.
▲ a scheme or systematic plan of action.
▲ includes setting measurable and achievable goals.
▲ asking, "How can we get this done?"

Edward Dayton and David Fraser, in their book *Planning Strategies for World Evangelism,* do an excellent job of illustrating what I have in mind. They explain the ensuing points about "strategy":

1. It gives us an overall sense of direction and cohesiveness. "Strategies, like plans, are road maps toward the future."
2. It forces us to see the mind of God.
3. It is a way to reach an objective.
4. It is an overall approach, plan, or way of describing how we will proceed in reaching our goal.

5. It is an attempt to anticipate the future.
6. It is a way of communicating our intentions to others (missionaries, local workers, supporters, area coordinator, regional director, general director, and the foreign missions board).
7. It helps us decide what we will do, and will not do. It excludes certain ways of doing things.

The following table is adapted from material taught by Dr. S. L. Poe with the Global Training Institute. It essentially shows that God provides the mission and the vision, while the strategy for its fulfillment is left largely in the hands of the recipient. The Lord of the harvest is interested in the strategy we use in fulfilling the vision.

Step one	God	Spiritual transformation	Paul was knocked down on the road to Damascus.
Step two	God reveals to man	Man receives God's mission.	
Step three	God assigns to man.	God provides vision.	God told Paul that he would be an apostle to the Gentiles.
Step four	Man decides the approach.	Man decides the strategy.	
Step five	Man continues the approach.		Paul's personality and talents came into the picture when looking at the program.
Step six	Action		God's plan required interaction with people. Action almost always brings us into contact with others.

Different tools are used for different tasks. Lloyd Shirley, the former director of education/AIM for Global Missions, wrote this in his annual report one year: "We've come to realize that the importance of a mission is determined by the ultimate impact it will have on the lost. . . . In retracing the years since 1972, it is clear that much has changed. It is also clear that the most important things remain the same. The task of balancing the changing and the changeless has always been a slippery slope to travel. John Stott said, 'It's easy to be contemporary if you don't care about being faithful. It is also easy to be faithful if you don't care about being contemporary.' In Global Missions we strive to hold on to unchanging truths.'"

The point is truth remains constant. God's principles remain timeless. Methods change. We need to be conservative enough to hold on to the truth, not neglecting it, or straying from it. Our efforts should never be in vain. We should be liberal or flexible enough to come up with new ways of presenting the gospel and God's Word to those in our generation, in a way they will be attracted to it. We can change the strategy.

Seasoned Supervision

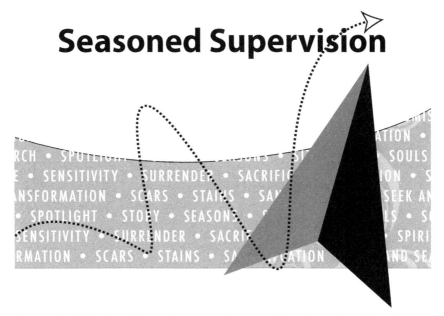

The will of God will stand up to the examination of spiritual men of God. They can give wise and godly counsel. Go to men who are mature and seasoned in the ministry. Private revelation will stand the test of public scrutiny.

The Bible has much to say about counsel.

- ▲ "Plans fail for lack of counsel, but with many advisors they succeed" (Proverbs 15:22, NIV).
- ▲ "Where no wise guidance is, the people fall, but in the multitude of counselors there is safety" (Proverbs 11:14, AMP).
- ▲ "Purposes and plans are established by counsel" (Proverbs 20:18, AMP).

Whom should you receive counsel from?

- ▲ Those who have made the journey before.
- ▲ Those who have your best interest at heart.
- ▲ Those who are spiritually-minded and can give good advice (Psalms 1:1-2).
- ▲ Those who are in spiritual leadership or authority over us.

▲ Those you trust.

What are the benefits of receiving counsel?

- ▲ Wise advice
- ▲ Confirmation
- ▲ Affirmation
- ▲ Mentorship
- ▲ Discerning questions
- ▲ Clarity
- ▲ Focus on the right path

Everyone needs three men in their lives:

Paul	Someone to lead you.
Barnabas	Someone to encourage you.
Timothy	Someone for you to mentor.

When Samuel heard God's voice, He heard it in the voice of his pastor, Eli. He went to his pastor for confirmation. His pastor gave him the right counsel.

Avoid people who:

- ▲ Tell you exactly what you want to hear.
- ▲ Always see it your way.

Watch out for ear-ticklers: "Instead, to suit their own desires, they will gather around them a great number of teachers to say what their itching ears want to hear. They will turn their ears away from the truth" (II Timothy 4:3-4, NIV).

Stand Still

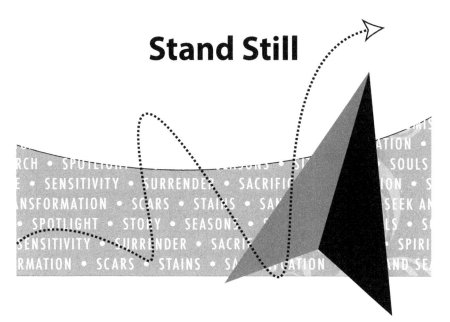

"I know thy works: behold, I have set before thee an open door, and no man can shut it: for thou has kept my word, and hast not denied my name" (Revelation 3:8).

Do nothing impulsively. "But they that wait upon the Lord shall renew their strength; they shall mount up with wings as eagles; they shall run and not be weary; and they shall walk, and not faint" (Isaiah 40:31).

"Fear ye not, stand still, and see the salvation of the Lord, which he will shew you today" (Exodus 14:13).

Wait!
by
Bruce A. Howell

We are born with an innate distaste and disgust for waiting. Perhaps it's an allergy. Babies enter the world insistently crying when they want to be fed, "I refuse to wait. I want food. Now!" We wait on our kids. We wait on our spouses. We wait in traffic. We wait in airports. We wait for church services to begin. We wait on latecomers for appointments. We wait!

Studies have determined how many hours or years of life we spend sleeping, eating, working; but I wonder how many hours or years, accumulated over a lifetime, that we spend waiting. Even now as I'm typing, my left foot is tapping the floor, as my toes wait for my fingers to catch up with my brain.

With overcrowded schedules and an endless list of things to do . . . today . . . we rush through the day. Occasionally revelation grips us. If only we had waited on the Lord in morning prayer, He would have ordered our footsteps. The day would have turned from fruitless and futile into fruitful and fulfilling. We sprint through life in such a hurry to live in the future that we fail to wait for it.

As I read through the Psalms, a light bulb was turned on, illuminating the word "Wait." It appeared first in Psalms 27:14, and it kept cropping up over the next dozen or so chapters. Could it be a sign? Probably not! More like a gargantuan thump on the side of the head.

"Wait for the Lord*! Be strong, and let your heart take courage: wait for the* Lord*!" (Psalms 27:14). "Be strong and let your heart take courage, all you who wait for and hope for and expect the* Lord*!" (Psalms 31:24, AMP). "Be still before the* Lord *and wait patiently for him" (Psalms 37:7). "But those who wait upon the* Lord*, they shall inherit the earth" (Psalms 37:9). "Wait for the* Lord *and keep his way, and he will exalt you to inherit the land" (Psalms 37:34). "And now, O* Lord*, what wait I for?" (Psalms 39:7)*

I've waited on a lot of things. Sometimes, patiently. More than sometimes, impatiently. Regardless, Scripture shouts, "Wait!" "Wait on the Lord!" What am I waiting for? Sounds like a reasonable question that longs for an answer.

1. As we wait, we stop all activity, focusing our undivided, undistracted, total concentration, and attention on God. He is bigger than all of our problems and circumstances. He comes with His still small voice and speaks into our situation.

2. Isaiah tells us when we wait on the Lord, we renew our strength (Isaiah 40:31). We get tired. We get tired of being tired. We reach the end of our rope and our abilities. It's there that we must stop and wait on Him to renew our strength.

3. We become united-in-heart with God (Psalms 25:21). The Hebrew word for wait *means "to bind together, as in twisting the strands of a rope." We become stronger when we wait on Him and incorporate His divine resources and power into our lives. When we refuse to wait, we run out of patience. It is there that we lose trust in Him.*

4. David confessed that He waited upon the Lord for deliverance to come. A couple of times as I meditated on this Scripture, email advertisements came through with the following words in the subject line, "The Battle is Not Yours! It Belongs to the Lord!" I've started getting the point! Especially when my name was inserted right before those words. To wait *is "to fix one's hope on God and anticipate His aid."*

5. "I wait for the Lord*, my soul waits, and in his word I hope. My soul waits for the Lord more than watchmen for the morning" (Psalms 130:5-6, NIV). I like that. God's Word is jam-packed with promises. You could claim one promise per day, for each day of your entire next term of missionary service, and not exhaust the long list of God's promises.*

6. Waiting is part of every missionary's or minister's ministry. We all are longing to "inherit the land." Don't be weary! Be faithful. You will reap a harvest. Faint not! To wait is defined as "staying in a place of hope until something expected takes place."

I want my testimony to be "I waited patiently for the Lord*!" (Psalms 40:1).*

Watch carefully the doors that begin to open. Open doors give guidance. We should approach an open door prayerfully. Not every door that opens to us is the will of God.

In God We Trust
by
Bruce A. Howell

Flip a coin or turn over an American dollar bill, and it is a comfort to find the words "IN GOD WE TRUST." When all is said and done, and we look for the bottom line, that line will be that God is our hope, and He always comes through for His people.

We trust God that He is big enough to save our world that exceeds seven billion people. I have seen Him at work in over 195 nations where the United Pentecostal Church International is represented. The UPCI reaches many cultures with one hope. Like someone said, "I've read the back of the Book, and I know who wins."

Revelation unfolds our anticipation. "After this I looked and there before me was a great multitude that no one could count, from every nation, tribe, people and language, standing before the throne and in front of the Lamb. They were wearing white robes and were holding palm branches in their hands. And they cried out in a loud voice: 'Salvation belongs to our God, who sits on the throne, and to the Lamb'" (Revelation 7:9-10, NIV).

Jesus came. He died. He rose again. He is our hope (Colossians 1:27). He is coming back for a triumphant universal church. That's a promise! The gospel will be preached in the entire world before He comes (Matthew 24:14). You can bank on that. In God we trust!

What's Your Destination?
by
Melinda Poitras

I was in a conference room not too far from here . . . on the floor. A group of MKs had gathered for the weekend, Philip Vannoy had just finished speaking about ministry, and I was feeling that feeling again. I think you know the one, the mind-numbing, heart-wrenching, soul- breaking burden for souls. It wasn't the first time I had felt it, and it won't be the last, but this day was different than the rest. The usual pictures began to flash through my head, and my heart over-flowed with love for the dark faces and dusty roads of my heartbeat—Africa. The only destination I thought I could ever care to visit, the place I had left indefinitely, the week before.

What now? I should have known a moment like that was coming. I had spent the year before working the best job I could hope for. It basically involved hugging little necks and reading deep educational material such as:

> You will come to a place where the streets are not marked.
> Some windows are lighted. But mostly they're darked.
> A place you could sprain both your elbow and chin!
> Do you dare to stay out? Do you dare to go in?
> How much can you lose? How much can you win?
> And IF you go in, should you turn left or right. . .
> or right-and-three-quarters? Or, maybe, not quite?
> Or go around back and sneak in from behind?
> Simple it's not, I'm afraid you will find,
> for a mind-maker-upper to make up his mind.
> (Oh, The Places You'll Go, *Dr. Seuss*)

I made up my mind, and shortly after arrived at Destination IBC, where I learned something about destinations in general. God doesn't promise that it will be easy, or fun, or that things will automatically go smoothly just because you're in His will. But you can rest assured that whatever the journey, when He picks your destination, it is always worth it.

Before I left Ghana, I sat down with our fellow missionary's daughter to try and explain what was going on. Five-year-old Allanah looked up at me with her big brown eyes welling up with tears and said, "I don't understand. Why would you leave?" And I told *her that there comes a time when everyone has to do something, and everyone has to go somewhere. That there are other places than this. Someone once defined missions as "joyfully advancing God's kingdom." That is exactly what each and every one of us is called to do. There is a big world out there full of people and places that need to hear about Jesus. Your world needs you.*

So...
be your name Buxbaum or Bixby or Bray
or Mordecai Ali Van Allen O'Shea,
you're off to Great Places!
Today is your day!
Your mountain is waiting.
So ... get on your way!
(Oh, The Places You'll Go, Dr. Seuss)

There are other places than this. Whatever the destination, Africa, Asia, Europe, or the United States. We all have to go somewhere. We all have to do something. What's your destination?